RECLAIMING THE GROUND

John Smith,
Paul Boateng, Bob Holman,
John Vincent, Hilary Armstrong,
Chris Smith

Edited by Christopher Bryant

RECLAIMING THE GROUND

Copyright © 1993 by Christian Socialist Movement
First published in Great Britain 1993
Second impression 1993

Spire is an imprint of Hodder and Stoughton *Publishers*

British Library Cataloguing in Publication Data

A catalogue record for this book is available from the British Library

ISBN 0-340-58857-8

All rights reserved. No part of this publication may be reproduced or transmitted in any form or by any means, electronic or mechanical, including photocopying, recording or any information storage or retrieval system, without either prior permission in writing from the publisher or a licence permitting restricted copying. In the United Kingdom such licences are issued by the Copyright Licensing Agency, 90 Tottenham Court Road, London W1P 9HE. The right of Rt. Hon. John Smith and others to be identified as the authors of this work has been asserted by them in accordance with the Copyright, Designs and Patents Act 1988.

Printed in Great Britain for Hodder and Stoughton Limited, Mill Road, Dunton Green, Sevenoaks, Kent by Clays Limited, St Ives plc. Photoset by Rowland Phototypesetting Limited, Bury St Edmunds, Suffolk.

Hodder and Stoughton Editorial Office:
47 Bedford Square, London WC1B 3DP.

In grateful memory of Canon Edward Charles, second
Chair of the Christian Socialist Movement 1975–83.
"One of the kindest, gentlest and most loving priests
they had ever known."

Contents

Foreword

Tony Blair was first elected MP for Sedgefield in 1983. He is a member of the Christian Socialist Movement and the Church of England. A barrister educated in Edinburgh and Oxford, he is now Shadow Home Secretary and a member of the National Executive of the Labour Party.

This book is not about using religion to advance a political party, or staking out a claim that one set of religious beliefs are superior to another. Neither is it an attempt to solve political problems by simplistic theological solutions. It is a book written by Christians who want to re-unite the ethical code of Christianity with the basic values of democratic socialism.

Like any great cause, Christianity has been used for dubious and sometimes cruel purposes wholly at odds with its essential message. But at its best, it has inspired generations of people throughout almost 2000 years to believe in and work for a better, more humane and more just world.

To radicals it has always had an especial validity. Radicals want change, and change, both personal and social, lies at the heart of the Christian religion. But it is change of a particular sort, based on a fundamentally optimistic view of human nature. It accepts the existence of our faults and our weaknesses; it is not in any sense Utopian. But it believes that there is a potential in human beings to do good that can be brought out and developed and made real.

Central to Christianity is the belief in equality; not that we are uniform in character or position, but on the contrary that despite our differences we are entitled to be treated equally, without regard to our wealth, race, gender or standing in society. It is about justice. Everybody should get the opportunity to make the most of themselves. The waste of human talent in our country and in our world today is an affront. It is shameful that millions of our fellow citizens are out of work, that many of our young people are left without hope and opportunity. And it is a brutal outrage that countless millions starve to death in a world that has abundance and plenty.

It is about compassion, the recognition that we will have to and should pay a price to help those less fortunate than ourselves, not as an act of charity to help them in dependency upon our bounty, but as a means of allowing them to achieve a better life for themselves.

It is about liberty, personal and social, freedom from unnatural restraint and freedom to enjoy and develop character and personality.

But above all, it is about the union between individual and community, the belief that we are not stranded in helpless isolation, but owe a duty both to others and to ourselves and are, in a profound sense, dependent on each other to succeed. This philosophy is sometimes used in such a way as to distinguish it from selfishness or even individualism. In one sense it is distinct from the notion of life as being about nothing more than personal acquisition or consumption. But this can give rise to a false choice between self and others. In reality the Christian message is that self is best realised through communion with others. The act of Holy Communion is symbolic of this message. It acknowledges that we do not grow up in total independence, but interdependently, and that we benefit from that understanding.

In political terms, this belief in community expresses itself through action collectively to provide the services we need, the infrastructure of society and Government without which modern life would be intolerable.

Therefore the values of democratic socialism, founded on a belief in the importance of society and solidarity with others, are closely intertwined with those of Christianity – hardly surprising in view of the Christian beliefs of many of the Labour Party's historical and present-day members. By rethinking and re-examining our values, and placing them alongside those of the Christian faith, we are able, politically, to rediscover the essence of our beliefs which lies not in policies or prescriptions made for one period of time, but in principles of living that are timeless. By doing so, we can better distinguish between values themselves and their application, the one constant and unchanged, the other changing constantly. To a Labour Party now undertaking a thorough and necessary analysis of our future, this is helpful.

However, it is also a powerful compass for the direction of change in our country. The new agenda in politics will reach out past old debates between economic ideologies of State control and *laissez-faire* and embrace different issues: the development of new economic opportunities for the individual; the environment, the third world, the international economy, the creation of modern, efficient public services. These issues must derive from some political values and we are as well to be sure of what they are.

A return to what we are really about, what we believe in, would be a healthy journey for our country as well as the Labour Party.

It would also help us comprehend more fully the importance of personal responsibility in our lives and its relationship to society as a whole. Christianity is a very tough religion. It may not always be practised as such. But it is. It places a duty, an imperative on us to reach our better self and to care about creating a better community to live in. It is not utilitarian – though socialism can be explained in those terms. It is judgemental. There is right and wrong. There is good and bad. We all know this, of course, but it has become fashionable to be uncomfortable about such language. But when we look at our world today and how much needs to be done, we should not hesitate to make such judgements. And then follow them with determined action. That would be Christian socialism.

Introduction

*Christopher Bryant is full-time organiser in the Holborn &
St Pancras constituency Labour Party, and Press Officer
for the Christian Socialist Movement. He is an ordained
member of the Church of England, and used to work as
Youth Officer for the Bishop of Peterborough.*

At first glance faith and politics have not tended to be very
good running mates. When publicly mixed together they
seem too often either to make for a rather distasteful,
garish and self-proclaiming campaign, or else to lead to an
explosive, intolerant crusade that takes no hostages. The
history of the world is littered with the casualties, real and
philosophical, of the battles for the moral high ground of
whatever faith. In this century Iran, Spain, Chile, Israel
and Bosnia have all witnessed the devastation that religious politics can wreak.

Even in democracies the combination has a bad track
record. In August 1992 we saw one of the most distasteful
political scenes of recent years. George Bush, standing for
re-election as President of the United States of America,
was determined to capture the Christian right wing by
portraying himself as the Christian candidate. He constantly referred to his own Christian faith. He ended
speeches with "God bless you all and God bless America".
He said that what was missing from the Democrat plat-

form was "G-O-D". He tried to capitalise on religious opposition to abortion and gay rights. Fortunately, however, soon after his Republican convention many of the Church leaders, including the Presiding Bishop of the Episcopal Church, Mr Bush's own Church, wrote to the White House pointing out that God was not a Republican, and might not even be American.

The ugliness of George Bush's attempt to pull the metaphysical rabbit out of the electoral hat was there for all to see. It was a low point in US history, a deliberate and cynical attempt to divert the electorate's attention away from the issues of the economy, the recession, social welfare, housing, law and order and unemployment, where the President's record was weak, on to the supposedly more favourable topics of supporting "family values" and patriotism.

Yet it was not an unusual form of political attack. In Britain, a nation less regular than America in its church-going, the Conservative Party has regularly attempted to portray itself as the party of the family, embracing traditional values, with its leaders very publicly attending church. Soon after being appointed Secretary of State for Education, John Patten argued that one of the reasons for an increase in crime was that too many young people had not heard of, or did not believe in, hell.

So in part this book is written in hesitation. All of the contributors are aware that it would be futile and immoral to claim God for one's own or for one's own Party. We are also aware that in presenting ourselves as Christian socialists we are running the risk of being seen as yet another set of politicians who want to capitalise on their faith and say, "I'm a Christian, so I expect all Christians to vote for me."

A Broad Church

The book, however, is also written in conviction, the personal conviction of eight people whose Christian faith has led us to espouse socialism. It is written in the conviction that faith has something to say to politics, and in particular to the Labour Party. It is written in the conviction that Christians, as well as other people of integrity, can and should be more involved in the decision-making of our nation, campaigning, putting themselves forward for election, trying to work for a fairer nation.

It is written too in the conviction that personal values cannot be neatly divided into moral and political, as so often seems the case in British politics. Supposedly there is a magical dividing line between those areas which are to be considered "moral", namely abortion, the death penalty, sex and religious education, homosexuality, Sunday trading, the age of consent, and those which are considered "political", housing, education, taxation, welfare and the economy. This book, though, is not restricted to the "moral", quite specifically because we believe that the political life of the nation is of a piece. Just as you cannot divide a person into separate pieces labelled material, spiritual and intellectual, so you cannot divide government into moral and political. Economic policy affects unemployment, which affects family life, which affects children's opportunity to reap the fruits of education, which affects their employability, which affects the efficiency of the economy. Government is a seamless garment, and this book is an attempt to weave a red thread through that garment.

It is also written in diversity. Some of those writing here believe firmly that a fairer society can only be achieved through a politics of altruism. Others argue that the Labour Party cannot simply demand sacrifice from the voters, the sacrifice of their ambitions, their aspirations and their pay. Some argue that individualism is the curse of modern British life. Others argue that the role of the Labour Party must be to champion the individual's freedom against the vested interest of big business, high finance, or unresponsive government.

The Labour Party

Above all, however, it is written in a tradition, for though the Christian Socialist Movement was only formed on January 22nd, 1960, there have been Christian socialists in Britain now for at least 600 years. Ever since John Ball, Wat Tyler's assertive priestly colleague, preached against Richard II in 1381 on the text "When Adam delved and Eve span/Who was then a gentleman?", there have been women and men inspired by Christian faith, prepared and determined to point out the inequity of the present political system and to advocate another based on justice and equality for all.

The central strand of this historical Christian socialism has always been that most acute of human sensibilities, the ability to perceive when something is unfair. It is the same sensibility that young people, even the five-year-olds as yet unhampered by the ideological clutter of their parents' society, exemplify when they shout across the playground, "It's not fair!" It is the same sensibility that inspired the Levellers, the Tolpuddle Martyrs, the social reformers of the nineteenth century, and the founders of the Labour movement. It is also the same sensibility as inspired the prophets of the Old and New Testaments to cry, "How long, O Lord, how long?"

If the central strand of this Christian socialism is a

moral concern for fairness, it is harnessed to an energetic will that the political system should be changed to one that is more in keeping with Christian ideals. Thus William Blake dreamt of building the concrete new Jerusalem "among these dark Satanic mills". Thus too Keir Hardie, the Labour movement's first Member of Parliament, and Charles Gore, the first Bishop of Birmingham and later of Oxford, both asserted that a society could and should be built upon the precepts of Jesus' Sermon on the Mount, with its emphasis on the poor, the hungry and those who thirst for justice.

So Christian socialism has always championed the poor. For some this has meant a very personal act of commitment, denying one's own comfort in order to work with and amongst the most vulnerable whilst campaigning for justice. Bishop Frank Weston put it this way when speaking in 1923 to the Anglo-Catholic Congress, "You cannot worship Jesus in the Tabernacle if you do not pity Jesus in the slum . . . Go out and look for Jesus in the ragged, in the naked, and in the oppressed and sweated, in those who have lost hope, in those who are struggling to make good."[1] Which is precisely what many clergy and lay people did, working and living in the slums of London, Portsmouth and Glasgow, not simply out of charity but in outrage that such conditions could exist whilst the disparity between rich and poor continued. For George Lansbury too, the Leader of the Labour Party and Poplar councillor, the personal commitment of living amongst those he sought to serve always underscored his political life. Thus a personal commitment always entailed a political will for change.

Before any of these, though, the modern history of Christian socialism effectively began with the launch of a series of pamphlets called "Politics for the People" in 1848.

The authors, Frederick Denison Maurice, Charles Kingsley and John Ludlow for the first time both accepted the title of Christian socialists and sought to achieve the "socialising of Christianity and the Christianising of socialism". It was John Ludlow who then in 1850 started the periodical *The Christian Socialist*, paid for in large measure by the philanthropist Vansittart Neale, and went on to initiate the Industrial and Provident Societies Act of 1852 which gave legal protection to all co-operative societies. In 1854 it was F. D. Maurice, who, having been turned out of his professorship at King's College, London, for his radical views, founded the Working Men's College at Great Ormond Street, with the support of Thomas Hughes of *Tom Brown's Schooldays* fame and Ruskin and Dante Gabriel Rossetti. Christian socialism had definitely been founded, and its impact was felt throughout the country with clergy and lay people campaigning for better water supplies, safer working conditions and more equitable pay. The Guild of Saint Matthew, under its leading light Stewart Headlam, went on to call in 1884 for "such measures as will tend . . . to bring about the better distribution of wealth created by labour".[2]

Reclaiming the Bible

One of the keenest influences of this early Christian socialism was the rediscovery of the Bible, not as a monumental tome to be abstracted from out of context, but as a historical document impregnated with truth. A coherent and much-neglected biblical theme was perceived, not so much urging sweet-hearted charity, but enjoining Christians to practise justice. In the Old Testament, it was argued, the prophets not only rounded on the rich who abused their privilege and bore scant regard for the poor, but they sought to uphold the Levitical code's attempt to "banish poverty from the land". So too the epistle of James condemned the rich and those who held back the pay of the hired workers overnight. Furthermore Jesus' ministry was clearly seen as the ushering in of a kingdom in which poverty would be no more. Frequently quoted was the parable of the sheep and the goats at the Last Judgement who are alike bewildered to hear the Christ welcome those who had fed the hungry, clothed the naked and visited those in prison, rather than those who had called him "Lord, Lord". Even in the Revelation of St John, with all its fiery symbolism, the enduring image of a new heaven and a new earth recalled Isaiah and the expectation of a renewed material world in which "no more shall there be . . . a child that lives but a few days" (Isa. 65:20 RSV). Victorian social concerns with child mortality, slum housing, vicious working conditions, and illiteracy, were all there in the Bible. The challenge for Christians and for a Christian society was to embrace and act upon the biblical understanding of fairness, or in more religious terms, "righteousness" or "justice", for, as Jesus taught in the Sermon on the Mount, "Blessed are those who hunger and thirst for righteousness, for they shall be satisfied" (Matt. 5:6 RSV).

This understanding of "justice" took people in many different directions. As we have already seen the co-operative movement largely achieved formal and legal recognition through the work of John Ludlow who believed in a society far more akin to the early Church where all things were held in common and the central religious act was the communal meal. The extension of common ownership to State socialism, however, was a more contentious matter. Thus Charles Gore, the editor in 1889 of the essays entitled *Lux Mundi*, and a founder member in the same year of the Christian Social Union, specifically denied State socialism as an aim, except in so far as it was right to oppose *laissez-faire* individualism. The driving force of the Christian Social Union, however, was Henry Scott Holland. He argued for a Christian economics in which common ownership was the only effective means of dismantling the privileges of inherited wealth and capitalism.

Feeding off both the Marxist analysis of capitalism and the profit motive and the ethical socialism of William Morris, he and others argued for the complete dismantling of capitalism, and for the progressive building up of alternative industrial systems. He quoted time and again Ezekiel's picture of the righteous person as someone who "does not oppress any one, but restores to the debtor his pledge, commits no robbery, gives his bread to the hungry and covers the naked with a garment, does not lend at interest or take any increase" (Ezek. 18:7–8 RSV). So justice had to involve very substantial economic change. Furthermore, because "Christianity is the most materialist of all world religions," as Archbishop William Temple was later to state, a Christian social order must bring material advance to all. It is only when co-operation, not competition, is at the core of the economic system that any significant advance can be made.

In the light of the Old Testament Wisdom tradition, and because of Jesus' own emphasis on teaching, biblical "justice" also meant for Christian socialists the wider dissemination of knowledge and education. After all it was often workers' lack of access to knowledge that had left them unable effectively to organise against unfair pay and working conditions. F. D. Maurice's Working Men's College in London was replicated all over the country and the adult education movement sprang from a passionate desire to combat illiteracy and spread knowledge, especially as technology advanced. The Socialist Sunday School, founded in 1892, with its "Socialist Ten Commandments" tried both to teach and to build solidarity, and its influence in many of the early Labour Party branches was immense.

Similarly, from the outset biblical justice could never be dissociated from peace. Just as Isaiah hoped that justice and peace would kiss one another, so Joel had enjoined the people of Israel to beat their swords into ploughshares (Joel 3:10). Jesus, the Christ, the "Prince of Peace", had listed the peacemakers in the Beatitudes. He had told his disciples to turn the other cheek, and refused to defend himself with weapons when the soldiers came to arrest him. This was an unequivocal witness that a Christian socialist had to take seriously. Thus in the first world war Keir Hardie was heartily opposed to granting the Liberals war credits to finance the conflict, and died a year after the start of the war, never having recovered from the deep shock to his belief in the internationalism of the socialist cause. George Lansbury agreed, "are we not taught that because Christ himself became flesh, therefore all life is sacred?"[3] It was an argument that he was to lose in the face of Fascism and the doctrine of a just war in 1935 when he resigned as Leader of the Labour Party. In later years the argument focused far more clearly on nuclear weapons. Christians such as Lord Soper and Bruce Kent were wholeheartedly involved both in the Campaign for Nuclear Disarmament and its Christian counterpart, Christian CND.

Bias to the Poor

Equality and the championing of the poor were also, of course, central to a biblical understanding of justice. Gustavo Gutiérrez, the Peruvian Roman Catholic priest, has pointed in his *Theology of Liberation* to the biblical understanding of poverty as embracing many different aspects. The Old Testament prophets almost universally condemn poverty as a sign of a society that has turned its back on God. They see the poor as those who lack food, water and a home, or as those who are oppressed by the wealthy, denied their rights, their wages or their land. They are to be championed because God made us all equal, and all are His children. The poor are also, however, seen in the Bible as the people to whom God is to come and the people from whom true wisdom will be known. Thus God frees the Israelites from slavery and leads them into the Promised Land. So too Jesus comes to the poor, deliberately picks the outcast for his allies and friends, and dies outside the city wall between two common thieves. He clearly asserts that it will be more difficult for a rich man to enter the kingdom of heaven than for a camel to pass through the eye of a needle. Gutiérrez then, along with many other liberation theologians and the Roman Catholic Bishops Conference in Puebla, believes that since God has made a preferential option for the poor it is incumbent upon the Church to do the same. The Anglican Bishop of Liverpool, David Sheppard, calls it God's *Bias to the Poor*. For the worldwide Church, especially in the developing countries where the majority of people lack the essentials of life, this theology of liberation has been the inspiration of the Basic Ecclesial Communities, working for justice, fighting dictatorships, speaking up for basic human rights and trying to build communal projects in the shanty towns of Lima and Nicaragua and the townships of South Africa. From this has sprung the work of Dom Helder Camara and Leonardo Boff in Brazil, Desmond Tutu in South Africa, Juan Luis Segundo in Uruguay and countless others.

For British Christian socialists God's bias to the poor has primarily been about striving for equality and an end to the rigid class system. Thus Josephine Butler worked in the nineteenth century with prostitutes, and Stewart Headlam with actors and actresses, arguing that no set of people was intrinsically more valuable than any other, and that indeed all were equal. George MacLeod used workmen from the Govan shipyards to supervise university students for the rebuilding of the ancient monastery on Iona, which was later to house his Iona Community. Kenneth Leech, at first working with young drug addicts in Soho and later fighting racism in Bethnal Green, constantly reaffirmed the incarnational belief in God's dwelling in all humanity and rejected the hypocritical stigmatising of sections of the community. The work of the Christian development agencies such as Christian Aid has also been about attempting to rectify the imbalance between the rich and the poor nations, putting an end to economic and theological neo-colonialism.

Undergirding all this has been a socialist critique of religion itself, spurring the Church on to tackle Marx's analysis of religion as the "opium of the people". Christian socialists have sought to put their theology in its social and political context, analysing the role of religion in society, and particularly condemning the false theology of "the rich man in his castle, the poor man at his gate; God made them, high or lowly, and ordered their estate" as in Mrs Alexander's hymn.

The Christian Socialist Movement

With all these variant strands, peace, co-operation, equality, economic justice and liberation theology, Christian socialism has rarely sought to present itself as a monolithic, dogmatic whole. What the foundation of the Christian Socialist Movement in 1960 represented was less an attempt to present a single coherent platform, and more an endeavour to give the Labour movement and the political scene in Britain a sense of moral vision and a vital agenda to tackle.

There was an informal manifesto, published on May Day, 1959, signed by Tom Driberg, John Groser, Donald Soper, George MacLeod and Mervyn Stockwood amongst others, and entitled *Papers from the Lamb*. Its title came from the name of the Holborn pub where Driberg and others had met regularly to discuss their faith and politics, rather than from theology. As a manifesto, however, it was less concerned with practicalities than with ideals, and so the movement set its agenda as it amalgamated the lay and clergy from the Society of Socialist Clergy and Ministers and the Socialist Christian League. As they say,

> these papers do not purport to give a comprehensive account of the Christian Socialist approach to all the problems of the day. It is felt, however, that they are worth publishing as a contribution to the discussion of some of these problems, and as an indication of the substantial measure of agreement that has been achieved between Christian Socialists of various points of view.[4]

So the Movement was founded, built on a firm foundation and incorporating many varying views, with Anglicans,

Methodists, Roman Catholics, Salvationists, Presbyterians and many other denominations as members.

Donald Soper chaired the Movement until becoming its President in 1975, and helped set its founding purposes, which have from time to time been changed and adapted. Since 1975 Chairs have been Canon Edward Charles and Peter Dawe. The Movement produces a regular magazine, and hosts lectures and residential conferences. It now embodies some 1,500 members and a number of local branches. In 1988 it affiliated to the Labour Party as one of the Socialist Societies, and now numbers amongst its members two of the Shadow Cabinet, twenty MPs, a Member of the European Parliament and countless local councillors.

R. H. Tawney

One of its most notable early members, and probably its most significant influence, however, was the Labour social historian R. H. Tawney. Born in 1880, Tawney was never elected to office within the Labour Party, nor was he ever to acquire a following as a great speaker, yet his legacy to the Labour Party was vital. Amongst other books he wrote *The Acquisitive Society* (1921) and *Equality* (1931). He drafted Labour's election manifesto in 1928 and 1934, and contributed ceaselessly to *The Manchester Guardian* and *New Statesman*. He was President of the Socialist Christian League from 1947 until the merger with the Society of Socialist Clergy and Ministers, and as such attended the inaugural meeting of the Christian Socialist Movement. Above all he was a critic of a society based on pure self-interest. He believed passionately in the dignity of people and the struggle for equality, arguing in 1912: "The essence of all morality is this: to believe that every human being is of infinite importance and therefore that no consideration of expediency can justify the oppression of one by another. But to believe this it is necessary to believe in God."[5] In later years he became a fierce critic not only of the Establishment and its vested interests, but also of the Labour Party and its leadership. Yet throughout his life, which ended in 1962, he sought to integrate his own personal commitment with the policies he advocated, offering integrity of vision, purpose and will to the political agenda. The *New Statesman* summed him up:

> Tawney, above all, embodied the vital, but elusive, element that has always distinguished the broad stream of British radicalism from the sectarian doctrines of European socialism – the belief that morality is superior to dogma and that the quality of people's lives matters more than their material achievements.[6]

Tawney's influence on the Christian Socialist Movement has long been acknowledged, and the Movement has held an annual lecture in his honour since his death in 1962. Four of the chapters in this book were delivered as Tawney lectures, those by Paul Boateng (1990), John Vincent (1991), Bob Holman (1992), and John Smith (1993). Previous lecturers have included Stanley Evans, Pauline Webb, Donald Soper, Tony Benn, Frank Field and Kenneth Leech, and ten of them were published in 1990 under the title *Fellowship, Freedom and Equality*.

It is then in a substantial tradition that this second book is written by Christian socialists. Above all though, it is written with vision. Gerrard Winstanley who tried to give his radical faith practical expression in the work of the "Digger" communities of the seventeenth century, wrote:

This great Leveller, Christ our King of Righteousness in us, shall cause men to beat their swords into ploughshares and spears into pruning hooks, and nations shall learn war no more; and every one shall delight to let each other enjoy the pleasures of the earth, and shall hold each other no longer in bondage.[7]

He spoke clearly then of a conviction which is held as strongly today. For not only does our Christian faith call us to believe in the equality of all, it also requires us to build a social system that knows how to husband the earth's riches responsibly in the best interests of all her citizens. As Christians we need personally and politically to create an environment for people to live in. That is to say an economic environment where people have access to adequately paid work; an urban environment that gives people places to live and spaces to recreate; a social environment where people have the freedom to develop their own and their family's full intellectual, emotional and spiritual potential; a world environment that gets food to people and gives them safety and security from war and disaster; a personal environment that enables people to form relationships that nourish them; a political environment that allows and encourages everyone equally to participate fully in the democratic process; and a religious environment that challenges us all, in the words of the prophet Micah, to "do justice, and to love kindness, and to walk humbly with your God" (Mic. 6:8 RSV).

BIBLIOGRAPHICAL NOTES

1. *Our Present Duty*, London, Church Literature Association, 1973.

2. A. J. Davies, *To Build a New Jerusalem*, London, Michael Joseph, 1992, p. 59.
3. *Ibid.* p. 118.
4. *Papers from the Lamb*, London, 1959.
5. "R. H. Tawney's Commonplace Book", J. M. Winter and D. M. Joslin eds, *Economic History Review* Supplement 5, Cambridge University Press, 1972, p. 67.
6. "A Man for All Seasons", *New Statesman*, 19 January 1962.
7. "New Year's Gift", Christopher Hill, *Winstanley; the Law of Freedom*, Cambridge University Press, 1973, p. 204.

1

Reconstructing the Common Good

Bob Holman is a neighbourhood worker on the Easter-house estate in Glasgow. He was Professor of Social Administration at the University of Bath and his books include his biography of George Lansbury, the Christian Leader of the Labour Party in the thirties, Good Old George. *He writes regularly for* The Guardian.

The post-war reforms of the Attlee government remain Labour's greatest achievement. The National Health Service, Family Allowances, Children's Departments, were established in the eventual context of rising employment. My grandmother had often expressed the fear, "Don't let me finish in the Union" (the provision of the Poor Law), so we rejoiced in the opening words of the National Assistance Act, "The existing poor law shall cease to have effect."

Accompanying these reforms was the large-scale council-house building. In places like Glasgow, huge estates went up, "deserts wi' windaes" as Billy Connolly called them. Unlike the privately rented slums, they had indoor toilets and bathrooms while the workers had jobs – the new Jerusalem.

All that has changed. I live in Easterhouse in Glasgow where now a third of the "economically active" are unemployed, and where 65 per cent of schoolchildren receive clothing grants, that is, they are from poor families. One in four flats is abandoned. Now the new Jerusalem is not desirable. However the common good is defined, this is not it.

Easterhouse possesses an unusually high concentration of unemployed and poor people but they are representative of the over three million unemployed and ten million poor people in our land. What is the explanation of this social malaise? The dominant explanation in the last decade has been popularised not by socialists but by the New Right. In this contribution I intend to examine New Right influence and then subject it to a Christian socialist critique. I shall then outline a Christian socialist version of the common good and consider steps to its attainment.

The New Right and the Underclass

During the early 1980s inner city riots and homelessness on the streets made social distress more visible. The New Right, by then the main influence on the Conservative government, began to produce its explanations. Most prominent was Charles Murray who, while acknowledging the existence of hard-working low-paid citizens, saw them being overtaken by an emerging underclass made up, mainly, of unemployed men and lone mothers. He portrayed them as lazy, irresponsible and often into drug abuse which they paid for by crime.

This underclass, to use Murray's language, is the product of the Welfare State which finances workless "barbarians" and "illegitimate babies". He writes, "the definitive proof that an underclass has arrived is that large numbers of young, healthy, low-income males choose not to take jobs."[1]

New Right politicians have latched on to the explanation. Michael Heseltine writes, "one of the more depressing aspects of urban life is a growing underclass."[2] "Growing", because its members breed children who grow up just like their undesirable parents. The underclass theory offers an explanation of poverty but it is not poverty that worries the New Right so much as the associated problems of unemployment, crime, drugs, public expenditure and the threat to traditional values. Just as Victorian politicians began to worry about the health of the poor once cholera threatened the middle classes, so the New Right politicians have worried that the example of the underclass might spread. Indeed, Murray fears that it is multiplying so rapidly that its "values are now contaminating the life of entire neighbourhoods".[3] And where does Murray see the classic example of the underclass neighbourhood? Why, Easterhouse, which is becoming a community without fathers where "the kids tend to run wild".[4]

The New Right Solutions

Following this analysis, the Thatcher and Major solutions have been straightforward.

- Firstly, privatise as much human activity as possible.
- Secondly, cut welfare spending.
- Thirdly, and in contrast to the language of freeing the market, enforce controls over so-called deviant individuals. Cuts in social security will force the unemployed to take low-paid jobs. Digby Anderson even wants the right to vote taken from the long-term unemployed.[5]

31

Murray says, "I want to re-introduce the notion of blame" so as to persuade young women to marry and look after their children properly.[6]

Influence on the personal social services

Clearly New Right doctrines have been applied to public utilities, the National Health Service, and to social security. Less recognised is its influence on the personal social services.

The government is pushing the services of Social Services Departments (Social Work Departments in Scotland) into the private market. Soon local authorities must produce Community Care Plans for "a mixed economy of care" with departments acting less as providers and more as contract makers with private and voluntary bodies. Social workers will be case managers who direct elderly and disabled people – and probably in the future needy children – to these agencies. The language employed implies that the users or consumers will have choice. But, as Bill Jordan warns, the power will really rest with the authorities who can select the agencies, and the agencies who can decide whether to bid for a contract.[7]

Accompanying these organisational changes have come changes in social work approaches to families in need. Faced with financial shortages and pressure to concentrate on child abuse, SSDs have most noticeably withdrawn from preventative work. To quote former SSD director John Rea Price, "throughout the seventies we used to do quite a lot to support parents. That preventative work was undermined. Social services departments have been putting all their resources into child abuse."[8]

In line with the New Right philosophy, social work has become, to cite Bill Jordan again, "more coercive and restrictive".[9] I went with a woman to a Social Fund

Review. When the official suggested she asked social workers for help her immediate response was, "No, they'd lift the weans". The New Right has engendered a social work of which some parents are scared.

Not least, social work now has top managers prepared to take £50,000 to run services for families receiving £9,000 or less a year. The New Right worship of personal gain has established itself even within social work.

Critique of the New Right

The New Right has reigned politically and the multi-million-pound Thatcher Foundation will attempt to maintain its kingdom. If the common good is to be reconstructed we must initially undermine the hold of the New Right. We do so because we believe its analysis and values are at variance with the truth. We do so as Christians, knowing, as Tawney put it, that a Church which remains silent in the face of State evil becomes "its apologist and its drudge".[10]

The New Right attributes growing unemployment, crime, immorality and poverty to an emerging underclass brought on by the Welfare State. Kirk Mann, in his devastating attack on Murray's scholarship, points out that the very vices and malaises of which he complains flourished even more fully in the Victorian hey-day of private enterprise when State welfare was almost unknown.[11] But let us concentrate on the present and turn to Easterhouse, Murray's classic example of a community overrun by this underclass of "irresponsible" young mothers and unemployed men. If Murray had examined the statistics, he would have discovered that 72 per cent of its children live in two-parent families – so much for a community without fathers. Further, the majority of those available for work are in employment, howbeit often in ill-paid job schemes, low-paid and part-time work. If he had lived in Easterhouse, Murray would have perceived that, although crime and drugs are serious problems, most families are opposed to them and most cope with their families in difficult circumstances. On a larger scale, Professors George and Howards, summing up the research, conclude that the values of socially deprived people are usually in line with the rest of society – although there are exceptions, "just as not all the middle and upper class individuals are motivated by exactly the same dominant values".[12] There is no separate and distinct underclass taking over Easterhouse or anywhere else. The underclass explanation is wrong.

Failed solutions

Given the faulty analysis, it is not surprising that the New Right "solutions" have failed. Services have been privatised. The market has been freed with tax cuts for the wealthy, the abolition of wage councils and tolerance of wages like £2 an hour for the unskilled. Social security benefits have virtually been withdrawn from 16–18-year-olds and the living standards of many Income Support recipients reduced. Life has been made even harder for the unemployed. At the Salvation Army hall near our flat, every day penniless families ask for cookers, beds, fires. And at the weekends the Sally's volunteers take food to those living on the streets.

Yet what has this mixture of privatisation and coercion achieved? The rate of economic growth has slowed, not accelerated, unemployment has risen, not fallen. Poverty has deepened. Crime has grown. It is early days to judge the effects of the contracts culture on the social services, but one study indicates it will lead to more bureaucracy and less efficiency.[13] In a letter to the Press, a reader tells of his efforts when told to move his bedridden mother from hospital. Social workers gave him a list of approved residential homes. Every one of them, when hearing the mother had no money and no property to sell, decided they had no vacancies.[14] The outcome in community care will be one service for the not-too-sick with financial means, and an inferior one for the very sick without cash.

Values

The New Right's analysis is faulty, but, as Christian socialists, our greatest disagreement is with its values. The New Right tolerates poverty and glories in inequality. Recently, a widow in Easterhouse – her husband killed himself after years of despairing unemployment – showed me her children's cold bedroom. It contained two beds, no other furniture, no radiator. By contrast, Mr Heseltine dwells in a £3-million estate of 400 acres with pheasants and trout lakes. Another woman upset her daughter by refusing to let her attend her friends' party because they could not afford a present. By contrast, Heseltine's London Docklands Development Corporation spent £100,000 on a party for its officials and VIPs. We condemn these inequalities as wrong in the sight of a God who created the earth's goodness for all, wrong according to the Son of God who taught that resources should be shared, wrong as alien to the divine intention of social cohesion not social division.

Further, our understanding of God who values all individuals and of Jesus who gave love to the despised and rejected is at odds with the total blame and harshness which the New Right directs at Murray's "barbarians". True, God gives individuals the power of choice, but He

35

also judges them according to their circumstances. When Jewish parents did the terrible act of selling their children, the anger of God's representative Nehemiah was directed not at them but at the money lenders who impoverished them. Similarly, as Christians, we see not barbarians but youngsters who are adapting to a life in which they have faced countless job refusals, grotty or non-existent training schemes, and little hope for the future. We do not believe that condemnation and coercion will be of any use to them.

Another explanation

If an expanding underclass is not the explanation, what is? My own studies, my observations in Easterhouse, lead me to concur with Professors George and Howards' review of the research,

> Advanced industrial societies are stratified along class, gender and race lines, so that economic and political power is unequally distributed. A person's economic position, and hence the risk of poverty, is decided largely by his family background, education, gender, race and occupation.[15]

People raised in socially deprived backgrounds are channelled into low-wage jobs or "giro careers" whatever their intelligence and values. By contrast, if at birth they had swopped places with Douglas Hurd, they would have been feather-bedded into privileged education and occupations. Of course, there are outstanding individuals who overcome disadvantages. I know an Easterhouse Ph.D. But these exceptions prove the rule in an area where in 1990 only one school leaver is reputed to have gone on to higher education.[16] Generally speaking, the people whom the

New Right condemns for their unemployment, poverty, life style, are the victims of a social system, not its cause.

Consider unemployment. In recent years, Western Scotland has been decimated by the closure of the shipbuilders, mines and now steel. Structural changes, not unmotivated individuals, have been the major reason for rising unemployment.

Consider child care. In 1984–5, 88 per cent of child care referrals to the Strathclyde Social Work Department came from low-income families. A mother called me in. She has struggled for years on Income Support. She has received an eviction order. The home is cold. She has made great sacrifices for her children and she loves them dearly, but she cried, "I can't go on!" These are not Murray's irresponsible parents. They are decent people caught in a system which undermines family life.

I am not putting forward an over-deterministic view of life. I am not denying the existence of evil amongst some poor people – nor amongst the rich. I am arguing that the British system structures some people into social deprivations. A few do turn to crime or break under the struggle. Most survive, howbeit at emotional and physical cost to their families.

And what is this system? Insufficiently controlled capitalism, which Tawney described as "the temper which is prepared to sacrifice all moral scruples to the pursuit of profit".[17] Under the New Right, the so-called free market has been reasserted as the mechanism by which resources can be unequally distributed and as a philosophy which blames its victims. The welcome collapse of Stalinism in East Europe should not be used to hide the fact that here the State is controlled by capitalism, not capitalism by the State.

During the last fifteen years, I have lived close to those

victims. Hence I go along with A. H. Halsey's summary of Tawney's position, "He saw capitalism not simply as un-Christian but anti-Christian."[18] It is as Christians that we must seek alternatives to New Right capitalism.

What is the Common Good?

If a new system is to be constructed, we must ask, what is the common good? Drawing heavily on Tawney's Christian socialism, I suggest it includes a society based upon the following.

Democracy
If all individuals are of value in the sight of God, then all should be enabled to contribute to the making of their society. This embraces, Tawney made clear, opportunities to partake in education, communication and politics. Further, it must also mean economic democracy. Tawney never advocated the nationalisation of everything down to the shoes on our feet. He wrote: "The idea of some Socialists that private property is necessarily mischievous is a piece of scholastic pedantry as absurd as that of those Conservatives who would invest all property with some kind of mysterious sanctity."[19] Tawney wanted ownership to be spread, whether via collective ownership or by the distribution of goods among individuals, so that economic power was not confined to a minority. Political and economic democracy must go together.

A society based upon proper relationships
Tawney then placed importance on all individuals enjoying the material abundance of God's world. Yet his criticism of twentieth-century Britain was also aimed at individualism and materialism. The rights of individuals

to amass material wealth and power had become the sacred cornerstone of the nation. The outcome was that powerful individuals became too egocentric, too self-seeking, regardless of the harmful effects on others. In so doing, things – that is, money, shares, property – become gods. "Such societies," Tawney explained, "may be called acquisitive societies, because their whole tendency and interest and preoccupation is to promote the acquisition of wealth."[20]

By contrast, Tawney called for a society which stressed, firstly, the proper relationship between people and material resources. The function of industry or resources should not primarily be the creation of wealth but the creation of services useful to the many. Tawney would reject Norman Lamont's 1991 assertion that "Rising unemployment and the recession have been the price that we have had to pay to get inflation down," because it ignores the effects of economic policy on the millions of unemployed – it is the wrong relationship.

Secondly, Tawney called for the right relationship between individuals, for which he used the New Testament term "fellowship". An individual may be created by God, but so are all individuals, and hence they possess a common kinship. Fellowship occurs when they relate to each other in recognition of common bonds and values. As Rose Terrill puts it, "Tawney's Fellowship implies a view of human beings . . . neither as gods nor as cogs, but as what Christianity knows as creatures."[21]

Socialism cannot enforce fellowship. It can place material resources at the service of people so that this proper relationship makes more possible the right relationship between people – fellowship.

A society based upon equality

Why do we want goods, services, opportunities, to be distributed equally, as far as possible? Because we believe that God created all people of equal worth. Tawney went so far as to say, "the necessary corollary, therefore, of the Christian conception of man is a strong sense of equality."[22] I need hardly add that being equal does not mean being identical, but rather implies a society, to cite Tawney again, "in which varieties of individual endowment, not contrasts of property, income and access to education, are the basis of differentiation".[23]

Democracy, Relationships and Equality

The Tory New Right has put back on the throne the kind of gods which the prophet Tawney tried to pull down. It is as Christians – though others, from different belief systems will agree with us – that we reject the acquisitive society and claim that the common good must be democracy, relationships and equality. I am not competent to explain just how these objectives can be reached. Instead, I will identify three components which are essential to it. Namely, we need to proclaim equality, we need to formulate policies which stem from our beliefs, and we need to practise socialism.

Proclaiming equality

An equal society is one not only in which members have access to similar resources and opportunities but also in which they value each other for their common humanity. Unfortunately, as Margaret Drabble explains, equality has "become a dirty word, a devalued word".[24] Under the sneers of the New Right, even Labour politicians have veered away from its use. Yet I believe we must popularise the concept of equality for these reasons.

Firstly, equality is essential to democracy. A country is not truly democratic if large sections of its population are, in reality, barred from its major institutions. As Jeremy Paxman explains in his *Friends in High Places: Who Runs Britain?*, Parliament, the Civil Service, the established Church, the City, the professionals, still draw disproportionately from a narrow élite.[25] The residents of places like Easterhouse are virtually excluded. Equality will entail the removal of both privileges and deprivations so that access is truly open to all – democracy.

Secondly, equality is essential if proper relationships are to be promoted. Human beings are not treating each other properly if some take incomes sufficient for needless luxuries while others have incomes insufficient for necessities. As Bacon put it, "Wealth is like muck. It is not good but if it be spread."[26] Further, fellowship becomes more likely within a context of equality. "Oh, no," the affluent liberal will protest, "I get on so well with my cleaning lady." Or, as a former colleague and radical once justified her exorbitant salary, "Now I can give more to the poor." But fellowship cannot flourish in enforced relationships. It requires the free choice provided by equality. As Tawney wryly put it, equality "will diminish the temptations of the rich, and make it somewhat easier for them to cultivate, in a practical form, the difficult virtue of fraternity".[27]

Equality is the fuel that drives people into democracy and the glue that bonds them in proper relationships. Our initial task in reconstructing the common good must be to popularise equality in our conversations, lectures, sermons, writings, so that it wins a place on the public agenda.

Policies Based on Beliefs

The New Right has used State money to promote élitist schools, weapons of mass destruction, private pensions. Michael Heseltine, while cutting local authority expenditure, launched the London Docklands Development Corporation which has received over £2.5 billion, mainly to stimulate private industry while removing aspects of local democracy. In short, the New Right carries through policies which reflect its values.

The next Labour government must fearlessly use public money, the people's money, on policies which stem from the socialist conception of the common good. In the long-term, this will mean a profound redistribution of income, wealth and power towards the end of equality. More immediately, and more within my sphere of experience, it can alter the shape of the personal social services and community involvement.

The personal social services and prevention

I explained that New Right influences on the social services have led to a more divided society with quality of service increasingly dependent upon income not need and with sections of the population treated as stigmatised outsiders. By contrast, Christian socialists should advocate personal social services which promote equality of service and greater social cohesion. It follows that we want welfare provisions which neither nanny people, nor coerce them, but which rather enable them to control their own lives and to contribute to the well-being of others.

Therefore, the primary function should be to support individuals and families in order to *prevent* them disintegrating into behaviour which gives officials grounds to remove them, against their will, from their families and neighbourhoods. Local authorities rightly have a duty to protect children and adults from abuse. As a former social worker I have exercised that duty. But protection now overshadows prevention. Significantly, the much vaunted Children Act of 1989 gives local authorities duties but not resources to support families. Paradoxically, prevention is decreasing not increasing.

In regard to families with children, the vanguard in each neighbourhood should not be teams of social workers but family centres with day care, play groups, youth clubs, welfare rights advice etc, available to the whole community, not just to the referred minority. These should be supplemented by social workers, family aides, home-makers and so on for those families requiring support within their own homes.

Children and adults needing residential care should be offered a range of services. Such services are too important to leave with the large commercial enterprises whose driving force is profit. They must be provided by local authorities supplemented by voluntary agencies whose motive is public well-being. Only then can the inequalities of a two-tier system be avoided.

Changes of this nature will need to be reflected in the staff of the social services. In particular, social workers should give up their drive to be *the* élite caring profession and instead share a standing with day care staff, home helps and welfare rights advisers in a service whose primary role is not to therapise clients or to monitor deviants, but rather to resource fellow citizens. Simultaneously, its leadership will require not abrasive chief executives in the entrepreneur mould but public servants who are not distanced by enormous salaries and luxurious surroundings from users of services.

George Lansbury spent forty years trying both to

improve and to destroy the Poor Law. He strove for social services which freed, not controlled people, services which the populace felt *belonged* to them. Only if our personal social services follow this path will they promote true equality.

The collective community

Outside the statutory social service is another world of welfare. Living in Easterhouse, I discovered that the most impressive forms of help consist in the coming together of low-income residents. Just in our small neighbourhood, I think of parents who run extensive play schemes, a tenants' association, a community association with an elderly persons' visiting scheme and a busy crèche for the under threes, a credit union for low-interest loans, a food co-op. I am employed by FARE (Family Action in Rogerfield and Easterhouse) whose members are made up of local residents.

These examples are typical of local action on the inner cities and peripheral estates. They receive little recognition but are significant for these reasons.

- They promote *participative democracy*. Community action involves people, who may steer clear of traditional democratic institutions, in collective decision-making in matters about their own neighbourhood.
- They demonstrate *the strengths of poor people*. Tawney explains that a turning-point for Beatrice Webb came when she stayed in a weaver's cottage and perceived that it was working-class men and women, "overworked, underfed and undereducated", who had created chapels, co-op stores and trade unions.[28] The New Right picture of an inadequate underclass is a falsehood. Community action reveals many to be citizens

who want neither to be controlled by politicians nor
cured by social workers, but who do want opportunities
and resources to use their abilities.

- They offer an *alternative to a profit-dominated market
economy*. Low credit, cheap food, stimulating leisure,
quality day care and jobs are provided by co-operative
effort. As a participant, I know that committees argue
and members disagree. Yet these members, often unemployed, often living in areas which the affluent
avoid, possess a spirit of fraternity based on proper
relationships. They do not relate as chief executive to
personal assistant, therapist to client, powerful to poor,
but as fellow members gathered for common ends.
Frequently, they share a fellowship which is absent
from organisations controlled by massive hierarchies
for the worship of Mammon.

For all their value, community groups remain the Cin-
derella of the social services. Central government will
donate to the headquarters of national charities with their
royal patrons and highly paid directors, but insists that
under-resourced local projects are the responsibility of
local authorities. Yet local authorities, themselves now in
financial straits, put them at the bottom of their priorities.
I work for an independent local charity which provides
advocacy for low-income families and clubs for 150 children a week on a total budget less than the salary of a top
manager. In eighteen months our voluntary funds will be
exhausted and I doubt if the local authority will enable it
to survive.

Communities
My proposal is twofold. Local authorities should give
priority to funding local groups which support families

and communities. Further, the next Labour government should establish a National Community Fund to be distributed directly to local groups by representatives from areas of high social need.

Such priority will actually enable local authorities to fulfil their preventative and supportive duties, for recent research by Gibbons, Thorpe and Wilkinson confirmed the hypothesis "that parents under stress more easily overcome family problems . . . where there are many sources of family support available in local communities".[29] Moreover, the expansion of community action will contribute to a society which displays democracy, proper relationships and equality.

The Practice of Socialism

The reconstruction of the common good will require a Labour government to base its policies on socialist principles. But socialism in general, and Christian socialism in particular, is not just about legislation. It is also about the way we live our lives.

In last year's R. H. Tawney lecture (see Chapter 3), Dr John Vincent explained that Jesus expected his followers to adopt his radical life style and so become "mini-embodiments" of the Kingdom of God. He then chided us for being comfortable socialists. This personal application now receives little attention, and even Roy Hattersley, who must have written on every other aspect of socialism, does not mention it in his *Choose Freedom. The Future for Democratic Socialism*.[30] Yet the equality of individual living is supremely important, for it is both a means and an end of reconstruction.

George Lansbury

In this last section I wish to take George Lansbury as an example of socialist practice.

Born in 1859, Lansbury spent nearly all his days in working-class East London, where he was converted to Christianity by the actions rather than the words of the vicar of Whitechapel. In turn, his understanding of Christianity took George and his beloved Bessie into socialism. As one of the first working-class Guardians, Lansbury substantially improved the Poor Law. As a Poplar councillor for forty years, he participated in municipal socialism. As a penniless man of faith, he helped found and then edited the *Daily Herald*. As a Labour MP, he was elected Leader when in 1931 the party was reduced to fifty-two MPs against 521. Michael Foot writes: "the rebuilding of the Party . . . was truly heroic; a combined feat of idealism and pragmatism, and George Lansbury was its embodiment."[31]

Lansbury's Christianity and socialism were not confined to church and chamber, but were expressed in his daily living. His *integrity* became a byword. He refused all bribes, perks, honours, even a Cabinet Minister's pension. In the LSE archives I came across the Lansburys' Co-op savings book at the time of Bessie's death and while George was leader of the opposition. They possessed £6.6s.3d. What a contrast with those MPs who use Parliament as a springboard to consultancies, directorships and lucrative posts in the media. Integrity.

Further, he chose to *keep close to those in greatest need*. He refused to leave 39 Bow Road for the suburbs and, consequently, ordinary men and women felt free to knock on his door even when he was a Cabinet Minister. Lansbury spoke with passion and perception because he lived alongside the unemployed and the socially deprived who regarded him as one of them.

Lansbury was in right relationships with people and hence he practised *fraternity*. Of course, he was not universally liked, and even within the Labour movement, the Bevins and Daltons sneered at his pacifist conscience. But overall his life is marked by the fellowship he experienced with those of similar values. In a few pages of his *My Life,* Lansbury refers to over sixty socialist friends, those like Docker Waite, who campaigned on an empty stomach, Charlie Sumner the hard-drinking stoker, and Mrs Savoy the brushmaker. The archives contain scores of letters from those who appreciated his kindness. No wonder A. J. P. Taylor called him "the most lovable figure in modern politics".[32] He was loved because he loved.

Lansbury is not unique. Mention could be made of Helen Born who, on becoming a socialist, moved to downtown Bristol to help unionise ill-paid women workers; Edward Charles, the former Chair of the Christian Socialist Movement, whom Kenneth Leech describes as "one of the kindest, gentlest and most loving priests";[33] Leah Manning, MP and teacher; Geoff Shaw, the minister who lived in the Gorbals and became the first convener of Strathclyde Regional Council; and others.

People who embody socialism are important for the following reasons. Firstly, they demonstrate that *socialism has a moral basis* quite different from other political creeds. These practitioners express beliefs in co-operation not competition, fellowship not division, equality not inequality. They must stop the Labour Party from adopting what Tawney called an electoral strategy based on a "glittering forest of Christmas trees with presents for everyone".[34] If the Labour Party loses its morality, it loses all.

Secondly, they show that *socialism involves more than winning elections*. Defeat at the polls does not extinguish

48

socialism. It can continue as a body of principles by which we attempt to shape our relationships with others no matter how difficult their political environment.

Of course, we want a Labour victory in order that the common good can be reconstructed. So, thirdly, *socialist practitioners draw others to socialism*. One of the features of George Lansbury was that he attracted people to his creed. Often this was through his public speaking in which, to cite Laski, he "lit a flame in a thousand hearts".[35]

Yet Lansbury was not a skilled or educated orator. As one of his colleagues, still living, wrote to me, "What he *was* was more important than even what he said." It is essential that the Labour Party wins not just votes but people to socialism, for, as Tawney warned, "The Labour Party deceives itself, if it supposes that the mere achievement of a majority will enable it to carry out fundamental measures unless it has previously created in the country the temper to stand behind it when the real struggle begins."[36]

In this discussion of Tawney I have tried to fuse practice and principle. Living in Easterhouse, I see daily the practical miseries resulting from poverty and inequality. I have argued that the New Right analysis and action, far from explaining these miseries, are a cause of them. Indeed, they have accelerated the development of a nation which, to use Keir Hardie's words, has "forgotten the centre cross and are worshipping at the cross of the thief".[37] In response, I put forward the objectives of a society based on participative democracy, proper relationships and equality, objectives drawn from our understanding of Christianity. To reconstruct the common good towards these ends, I suggest policies which stem from our beliefs, policies which will radically redistribute society's resources, which will build personal social services which are open to and belong to all citizens, and which develop the fraternity and strengths which are available in our communities. Finally, I state the paradox that this social revolution cannot be separated from everyday socialist living. We want a reconstructed society so that it becomes easier for individuals to share goods, emotions and friendships. Yet it is partly the quality of our present socialist lives that must convince others that reconstruction is necessary. As always, Tawney has already said it, "Socialism has two aspects. It implies a personal attitude and a collective effort. The quality of the latter depends on the sincerity of the former."[38]

Tawney admired George Lansbury because the latter, with none of Tawney's social and educational advantages, managed to put the individual and the collective together. So let Good Old George have the last word,

It is useless to sing of fraternity, just simple nonsense to write of comradeship and love, unless we are willing to forgo all idea of material and economic superiority, and to find our greatest reward in the fact that we have served our fellow men and women.[39]

BIBLIOGRAPHICAL NOTES

1. C. Murray, *The Emerging British Underclass*, London, Institute of Economic Affairs, 1990, p. 17.
2. M. Heseltine, *Community Care Lecture*, 1990.
3. C. Murray, *op. cit.* p. 4.
4. C. Murray, *op. cit.* p. 12.
5. D. Anderson, *The Sunday Times*, 30 September 1990.

6. C. Murray, *op. cit.* p. 71.
7. B. Jordan, *Social Work in an Unjust Society*, Brighton, Harvester Press, 1990, p. 3.
8. J. Rea Price, *The Guardian*, 17 September 1991.
9. B. Jordan in P. Carter et al. (eds), *Social Work and Social Welfare*, Oxford University Press, 1991, pp. 23–4.
10. R. Tawney, *Religion and the Rise of Capitalism*, London, Pelican, reprinted 1948, p. 196.
11. K. Mann, *The Making of an English Underclass*, Oxford University Press, 1992, p. 107.
12. V. George & I. Howards, *Poverty Amidst Affluence*, Aldershot, Edward Elgar, 1991, p. 108.
13. *Contracts at the Crossroads*, Association of Crossroads Care Attendants Schemes, 1991.
14. Letters to the editor, *The Guardian*, 10 October, 1991.
15. V. George & I. Howards, *op. cit.* p. 93.
16. Reported in "Workwise Working" (unattrib.), *Scan*, July 1991.
17. R. Tawney, *op. cit.* p. 93.
18. A. H. Halsey (ed.), *Traditions of Social Policy*, Oxford, Blackwell, 1976, p. 249.
19. R. Tawney, *The Acquisitive Society*, London, Fontana, 1961, p. 82.
20. *Ibid.* p. 32.
21. R. Terrill, *R. H. Tawney and His Times*, London, André Deutsch, 1973, p. 218.
22. R. Tawney, *The Attack and Other Papers*, Nottingham, Spokesman Books, 1981, p. 182.
23. *Ibid.* p. 60.
24. M. Drabble, *The Case for Equality*, London, Fabian Society Tract 527, 1988, p. 1.
25. J. Paxman, *Friends in High Places*, London, Penguin, 1991.

26. Cited by Tawney in *The Acquisitive Society*, *op. cit.* p. 54.
27. Cited by Terrill, *op. cit.* p. 197.
28. R. Tawney, *The Attack*, *op. cit.* p. 104.
29. J. Gibbons with S. Thorpe and P. Wilkinson, *Family Support and Prevention*, HMSO, 1990, p. 162.
30. R. Hattersley, *Choose Freedom. The Future for Democratic Socialism*, London, Michael Joseph, 1987.
31. Cited by B. Holman, *Good Old George: The Life of George Lansbury*, Tring, Lion Publishing, 1990, p. 147.
32. Cited by B. Holman, *Good Old George*, *op. cit.* p. 181.
33. K. Leech, "A truly political point", *Christian Socialist*, Winter 1991/2.
34. R. Tawney, *The Attack*, *op. cit.* p. 57.
35. Cited by B. Holman, *Good Old George*, *op. cit.* p. 178.
36. R. Tawney, *The Attack*, *op. cit.* p. 66.
37. E. Hughes (ed.), *Keir Hardie's Speeches and Writings*, Foreward Co., n.d., p. 37.
38. R. Tawney, *The Attack*, *op. cit.* p. 58.
39. G. Lansbury, *These Things Shall Be*, Swarthmore Press, 1920, pp. 67–8.

2

The Hope of Things to Come

Paul Boateng first made his mark as a civil rights lawyer in London in the 1970s, and having been elected MP for Brent South in 1987 he is now the Shadow Spokesman on the Lord Chancellor's office.

Hope has two beautiful daughters. Their names are anger and courage; anger at the way things are, and courage to see that they do not remain the way they are. *St. Augustine.*

The Labour Party owes more to Methodism than to Marxism and no wonder, for the good news that Christ proclaims to the world challenges us to transform ourselves and our institutions in a far more radical way than Marx ever did.

Anyone looking to the Gospels, however, for a simple endorsement of a set of political prescriptions or the ultimate in Labour Party manifestos of yesteryear, long on prose and short on practicalities, will be disappointed.

Christians down the ages have faced persecution for the reason that Christ is not to be co-opted on to anyone's policy committee. Our faith is deeply subversive, it puts the human spirit before institutions and subordinates the powers and the principalities to the overriding principles of love.

The Cry for Justice

Christ rules OK and love passes from sentiment to a strategy that works for the end of unjust rule and the coming of the kingdom.

> We now pray that God will replace the present unjust structures of oppression with ones that are just and remove from power those who persist in defying his laws, installing in their places leaders who will govern with justice and mercy. The present regime together with its structures of domination, stands in contradiction to the Christian gospel to which the churches of the law seek to remain faithful.
>
> We pray that God in his grace may remove from his people the tyrannical structures of oppression and the present rulers in our country who persistently refuse to hear the cry for justice.
>
> We pledge ourselves to work for that day.
>
> A. A. Borsak and C. Villa-Vicercin,
> *When Prayer Makes News*, Westminster Press, 1986

So ran the call to prayer of the South African Council of Churches to make Sunday, June 16th, 1985 Soweto Day.

When I first visited that country in 1988 I found churches in Soweto and the Southern Cape that were surrounded by barbed wire and caspirs. The liturgy and songs of praise that have come from the struggle waged there have cast a new light on worship throughout the world. White youngsters in places of Christian worship in our country sing "Si Ya Hamba . . . " (We are marching in the light of God). The anthem of the ANC "Nkosi Sikelel'i Afrika" is a hymn written by Enoch Sontonga for a Methodist ordination for all the peoples of that land, black and white, meaning – God bless Africa.

The Church and the people of God have also been in the forefront of the struggle for justice in Latin America and what was the Soviet "Empire". The churches in East Germany were at the heart of the resistance to Marxist tyranny in that country. They now face a new challenge from the corrosive materialism of the market that has replaced the monolithic Statism of the past.

We who confess Christianity and profess our socialism face a real challenge in the world today. We know that the satisfaction of material needs alone does not bring fulfilment. We also know that poverty and the human and environmental degradation that accompany it are a gaping wound in the body of Christ. We are called to heal that wound and to provide a context in which the spirit may grow freely towards unity with Christ.

Kwame Nkrumah, leader of Africa's first black independent state, Ghana, used to say, in the context of the struggles for colonial freedom, adapting and turning around the gospels, "Seek ye first the political kingdom and all things will be added unto it." The cause was of course just but he was profoundly wrong. The political kingdom is, at best, only ever a mirage and at worst an all too real tyranny unless at its heart is the metropolis of the spirit.

Love in Action

The metropolis of the spirit is the city of God. Our God is a God of justice who is on the side of the oppressed, the poor, the orphaned, the sick and the alienated. Our God made the world as a beautiful place and gave man and woman responsibility for it, made us to live, not only in intimate relationship with Him, but in community together. Our God is not a Moloch, he does not demand our children as a sacrifice. He gave us His child that we might have eternal life.

He loves us unconditionally, but the nature of that love requires that we open ourselves to it. We have a choice. The power of His love enables us to transform our own lives. There is, however, still more to this love that we call the Holy Spirit. This is its capacity, through our prayer and action, to transform the institutions of which we are a part and the world in which we live. There is an imperative for Christians to address the injustice that is so wounding to Christ and destructive of His creation. Jesus sets our agenda for us at the beginning of His own ministry, in this way in Luke 4:18–20 (NIV):

"The spirit of the Lord is on me,
because he has anointed me
to preach good news to the poor.
He has sent me to proclaim freedom for the prisoners
and recovery of sight for the blind,
to release the oppressed,
to proclaim the year of the Lord's favour."

Love, therefore, to us as Christians, goes beyond sentiment to require us to formulate a strategy. The strategy needs to meet not only the requirement of the spirit but the world's material needs. The fate of those who claim to follow God and neglect this is graphically described in Amos 5:11–12, 14–15 and 21–24 (NIV).

You trample on the poor
and force him to give you grain.
Therefore, though you have built stone mansions,
you will not live in them;
though you have planted lush vineyards,
you will not drink their wine.
For I know how many are your offences and how great
　your sins.

You oppress the righteous and take bribes
and you deprive the poor of justice in the courts.
Seek good, not evil,
that you may live.
Then the LORD God Almighty will be with you,
just as you say he is.
Hate evil, love good;
maintain justice in the courts.

"I hate, I despise your religious feasts;
I cannot stand your assemblies.
Even though you bring me burnt offerings and grain
　offerings,
I will not accept them.
Though you bring choice fellowship offerings,
I will have no regard for them.
Away with the noise of your songs!
I will not listen to the music of your harps.
But let justice roll on like a river,
righteousness like a never-failing stream!"

Christian Realism

How then do Christians in a socialist party witness their faith and how do socialists in a Christian church conduct themselves? We have first to face up to some truths. Socialism in Britain, like the Christian Church, seeks an urgent renewal and a clearer vision. Membership is falling. Cynicism, apathy and hopelessness hang like a pall over the nation. Many wish it were otherwise and seek a way forward into the next millennium. There is hope to be found in this search.

Socialists ought not to seek refuge in the past. Ours is surely a view of the world that is based on the world as it is and seeks to transform it, not as it was or might have been, but to what it could be. The notion of the Big Daddy State is largely discredited, even as the overriding wisdom of the market is revealed as a mechanistic nonsense. The State should be seen neither as a paria nor as a primary provider but as an enabler and empowerer. A new contract between the State and the individual is called for based on community as well as individual rights and responsibilities.

Christians, on the other hand, must not fall prey to pietism and a fatalistic individualism. There is a heresy currently observable and gaining ground, in some areas of Christendom, that material wealth is, of itself, a sign of grace. This finds its obverse in the belief to be detected in some quarters on the Left that the redistribution of wealth is, of itself, the precursor to the coming of the Kingdom. This is false coinage, however brightly it may shine or however common its currency. The way forward lies elsewhere.

We ought perhaps first to seek some guidelines for Christian involvement in political and economic issues

and the struggle for justice. I would tentatively suggest
the following:

Followers of Christ cannot partition religious life and
worship from involvement in the concerns of political and
economic justice. Life isn't to be separated into little boxes
in this way, one labelled religious and the other secular.

Hope for the Poor

As Christians we have to recognise the nature of Christ,
King and Saviour yes, but of unique sort, arising out of
and himself one of the poor. We have, therefore, to stand
alongside the poor if we are to be close to him.

Jesus himself says so, our treatment of the marginalised is of eternal significance: "Depart from me . . .
For I was hungry and you gave me nothing to eat, I was
thirsty and you gave me nothing to drink, I was a stranger
and you did not invite me in, I needed clothes and you did
not clothe me, I was sick and in prison and you did not look
after me . . . whatever you did not do for one of the least of
these, you did not do for me" (Matt. 25:41–43, 45 NIV).
The Christian imperative is that systems and institutions
be opened up not only to be inclusive of the needs and
aspirations of the poor and the marginalised, but also to be
judged on how far they themselves are able to participate
actively in them.

All Christians are subject to a moral agenda by which
legality can never be an ultimate ethical principle.
Rather, to be morally justifiable, laws must be sustaining
of life and liberty, and where they are not, civil disobe-
dience and non-cooperation are not only themselves justified but may become obligatory. The lives of Pastor
Niemöller in Germany and Dr Martin Luther King in the
United States and Wolfram Kistner in South Africa all
bear witness to this.

Christians have no choice over whom we love. Our concerns for justice must embrace all. We must look beyond the boundaries of race, class and nation. Of necessity then we must reject the politics of envy and hate, challenge prejudice and go beyond narrow sectional or national interest to a vision of global economic and political justice.

The practical implications of such guidelines on political life are startling. This is no reason to reject them. On the contrary, for the guilt and powerlessness which our failure to live up to them might otherwise create in us is overcome by the knowledge of this fact: Christ died for us and loved us. Confidence in this and his presence amongst us is the surest antidote to the pessimism that paralyses action and prevents us from standing up for good and against evil. We have the certainty too, that only in the second coming of Christ will his ultimate victory be assured. This ought to stop us from having unrealistically high expectations of any political structure or economic system. Even in a better dispensation than that we currently endure, Christians would need to be constantly striving for justice.

Justice and the Health Service

Capitalism relegates faith to the arena of the purely personal. Marxism banishes it to the margins of superstition. Both, with cause, feel threatened by the notion of the Spirit at work in the world. The challenge to those who confess Christ and profess socialism is to integrate the material and the spiritual.

What are the implications of this for practical policy? The health service is an area of acute political controversy. The debate between market and socialised medicine all too often becomes one dominated by the issue of how to raise the resources required to finance the health service. This is, of course, important but not the only issue, nor necessarily the primary one. The Thatcher era witnessed the transfer of power within the NHS from the consultants to the accountants. The Labour Party has to offer more than a reversal of this process. Christians can help in this. Applying the guidelines I have briefly outlined, we need to test the development of a policy against the criteria which they indicate for successful, life-enhancing institutions.

A key issue, and one that requires to be addressed urgently, is where power lies within the NHS. An institution capable itself of surviving and sustaining the life and health of those it serves ought to be about extending power, not only to junior doctors, nurses, ambulance staff, paramedics and ancillary workers but also to patients. Why is it that so little attention is given to the sense of powerlessness that descends on the patient when entering hospitals and that is reinforced everywhere by the practices and procedures adopted there? Why is the experience of women in the field of birth and gynaecology so often one of being part of some production line in which they are required to surrender control over their own bodies to men in white or green? Why is so much attention given to spare-part medicine and so little to a holistic approach to treatment? Why for dignity in death is it so often necessary to go outside the health service altogether to the hospice movement? A socialist policy which seeks to address these questions overcomes the response, "Where is the money coming from?" by meeting people's concerns about the nature and quality of the service, which the market is incapable of addressing.

The Creation of Wealth

The creation of wealth and, therefore, the availability of
the resources whose more equitable distribution we seek
is an issue that we must address as Christians and socialists. A failure to do so involves a surrender of territory to
forces that work against justice and equity. This may be
more comfortable, particularly as it leaves us free from
the need to address our own position cocooned in a network of power and economic relations that insulates us
from the shock of Christ's imperatives, but it is neverthe-
less ultimately an untenable one. How much easier it is,
however, in the short term, to rail at the self-interest of
others, to scorn the mucky business of making and selling
things and at the same time to wring our hands at the
dilemma of persuading others to vote for tax increases. We
all too often seek the assurance of eternal life, a Labour
Government everlasting and not so much change as to be
uncomfortable and frighten the voters. This is the path to
disappointment.

Jesus warns against the dangers of wealth but does not
absolve us from the responsibility of its creation. The
challenge lies in the means of its generation and the use
we subsequently make of the wealth we have created.
When the rich man asks what he can do to ensure eternal
life, Jesus tells him to distribute his money to the poor.
But Jesus' response to his listeners when they ask who
might be saved if it is thus so hard for the rich, is not the
easy and obvious one – "Why the poor and the powerless,
of course" – rather, that "What is impossible with men is
possible with God" (Luke 18:26–27 NIV). Everlasting life
is therefore Godgiven and accessible to all. Hating the rich
and making them squeal is not a part of that answer. Pie
in the sky when you die is not meant to assuage immediate

pangs of hunger or remove the responsibility for addressing these in the here and now; on the contrary, the promise of life everlasting demands that we do just that.

God's love is unconditional but, as in Saint Teresa of Avila's prayer, what hands and feet, eyes and ears does He have other than our own? God provided His people with manna but the people in turn were called to collect and distribute it and to avoid waste and profligacy in so doing.

How are we then to approach the business of wealth creation? We begin by recognising our responsibility to address the issue from a Christian perspective. Exploitation and confrontation and a view of economics that subjugates humanity to the mechanistic workings of forces deemed outside our control are not compatible with a Christian ethic. Is it really true, in any case, that the failure of the British economy is due to the corrosive effect on the competitive spirit of British firms by anti-market forces? Is it really the case that Thatcherism hasn't delivered because we haven't been Thatcherite enough? Is there still too much regulation, too much taxation and too little flexibility in price and wage determination policy? Or might it just be that the *laissez-faire* prescriptions of the 1980s, which continue to have the leadership of the Conservative Party and a substantial body of British economists in their thrall, were just plain wrong?

Mrs Thatcher sought in her address to the elders of the Church of Scotland to claim theological justification for these policies in the commonplace misreading of the parable of the talents. The elders, whose grasp of theology is considerably greater than Mrs Thatcher's grasp of economics, were unimpressed. They had every reason to be, but not only on theological grounds.

The free market

Christians who profess socialism are entitled to take a view that is based on a very different interpretation of scripture. The prophetic vision of the Old Testament and the witness of Christ's life in the New, place the emphasis of a Christian life beyond the individual and his or her self-interest, to embrace the welfare of the community as a whole. Co-operation and a shared responsibility by both individual and corporate bodies, rather than confrontation and an abdication of corporate responsibility, are shown as the way forward.

The Christian ethic recognises a duty on the part of individuals to come together in society to share responsibility. The notion that there is no such thing as society is therefore profoundly anti-Christian. We are held collectively to have a duty to protect the weak, just as we have a duty to protect God's natural creation from the depredations of our industry. This is not to deny to all the opportunity to participate in accordance with their skills in a dynamic and productive society.

True liberty, choice and opportunity require nurturing and do not arise spontaneously from the absence of discipline and regulation. There is every reason to believe that an economy run along those lines is likely to produce wealth more effectively than a prostrate obedience to the Moloch of market forces. The unregulated free market is truly a false god in that it does make seemingly insatiable demands for the sacrifice of the work and life opportunities of more and more of our citizens in order to satisfy the appetites of a few.

The economist Will Hutton makes the point very well in reviewing the impact of the prescriptions of Conservative economic policy in its attitudes towards the firm and wealth creation over the past decade. He makes the charge that the firm, as an instrument of wealth creation, is not as simple in its nature and responses as market economists would have us believe.

> In essence the firm is being seen as a social organisation embedded in a network of other organisations, and the surrounding legal, financial and institutional framework means that price signals do very different jobs in different settings.
> In particular, a key determinant of firms' strategies and internal control systems is the pattern of ownership of the firms' shares, and the signals shareholders send to the firms' managers. Rather than too little exposure to markets, companies can have too much exposure to the wrong kind of market pressure, the kind that highlights risk and undermines enterprise. And as these forces are reproduced throughout the economy the enfeeblement is general.

There is, therefore, a strong case for an important intellectual reappraisal of what makes firms work. Germany and Japan have some lessons for us in this respect, as their capacity to weather the global recession better and to maintain and develop a stronger manufacturing base than our own indicates. Britain's slavish addiction to the free market, the constant battle waged by Government against organised labour, and the climate of fear in industry arising from the threat of takeover, restructure and shrinkage have all contributed to our decline, not only in employment but in economic vigour.

Vision for Renewal

Christians and the Labour Party must not shrink from taking part in the processes of this reappraisal. Enterprise, choice and opportunity and the language of economic success must not be seen as a no-go area for Christians any more than for socialists. We must not shrink from the dynamic of wealth creation and the arguments around it for fear of getting our hands dirty. To transform, we must first engage.

There is much to be done but we have an opportunity in the next few years to bring to a conclusion the process of review that began several years ago in the Labour Party, with a vision that is based on a genuine renewal of our spirit and nation. Christ teaches us to see with the eyes of our heart. Paul's prayer and intercession on behalf of the Christians at Ephesus and in Asia Minor, who found themselves in conflict with forces that appeared to dominate the world, was that God might give them "enlightened eyes of the heart" so as to know what was the hope of their calling. May our eyes also be so opened.

3

Jesus as Politician

John J. Vincent is Director of the Urban Theology Unit in Sheffield. He was President of the Methodist Conference 1989–90 and his books include Radical Jesus, Christ and Methodism, *and* Into the City. *He writes regularly for* The Guardian.

The Search for the High Ground

In his Preface to the first ten Tawney lectures, *Fellowship, Freedom and Equality*,[1] David Ormrod observes that in recent Tawney lectures, socialism as the major preoccupation has been replaced by pressing immediate agendas – development, political economy, justice, race, third world issues, communication, struggles for liberation. There has been a tendency to leave "larger questions" for the sake of attempting to push back the frontiers of injustice, consumerism, capitalism, State control, or whatever, in favour of seeking some kind of redress or justice or equality at society's most vulnerable points.

Inevitably and properly, Christians and socialists and Christian socialists are still trying to find their feet after a decade of worldwide white Western reactionism, "New Right" philosophy and, in Britain, monetarism and market-forces Toryism. Naturally, we seek to oppose the erosion of hard-won rights and privileges available to all. However, we are perhaps in danger of letting our enemies write the agenda. And by so doing, we neglect the constant need to re-create for every new generation a distinctively Christian approach to the whole of national life. So in this chapter, at any rate, we shall go for the "commanding heights", or some great principles, particularly some Christian political bases.

Yet to attempt to do so in the 90s means that we have to start rebuilding the foundations of Christian political thought and action almost from nothing. I am not competent to do this in the sphere of political theory, let alone party politics. I have lived through decades in which the great slogans of the political Left have been taken over by the other side. Freedom has become freedom of opportunity. Equality has become equality in being able to acquire as much as we like. Democracy means winning over as many as we can to believing their private interests will be best served by the party. Meantime, Marxism as a useful tool has taken a battering. And "New Marxism" is a new enlightenment still seeking some practicalities. Inevitably, one has to ask, what is the shape of socialism in the twenty-first century? That is a question urgent for answers. Those concerned with it need to get some ideas out soon, I judge.

But there is also a task at the other end – to attempt to state the Christian or theological side of a Christian political ideology and vocation in terms which make sense today. That is the task I shall venture to begin.

Britain in the 90s

That the need is for precisely these endeavours I have no doubt. During my year as President of the Methodist Conference, 1989–90, I spoke at six meetings in the House of Commons on the theme "Britain in the 90s". The responses varied greatly – and at times some of the meetings generated more heat than light. But there was a strong underlying theme, expressed by many MPs of different parties.

It went something like this. "Yes," they said, "it is important to deal with immediate issues. Yes, we must oppose injustice, and name it where necessary. But such tasks do not get to the root of things. They are the necessary watchdog function of Christian conscience. But they are not the reasons most of us came into politics. We came into politics because we had some overarching vision that we could actually help create a better Britain – whatever that might mean.

"And, especially, we who are Christians in the House" – between 100 and 200 are churchgoers, they said – "we need to be constantly called back to a debate about the high ground of British politics, about what we are here for, what we are serving and what our aims and objectives are. It is not that we shall necessarily agree on such things. But at least we shall be debating matters more long term than the rights and wrongs of particular pieces of legislation, or the means whereby this party or that takes up its party political positions, and uses us to win its battles. And with that larger task," they said, "the Churches and the theologians have not been very helpful."

So, then, how can the Christian springs of political responsibility be restated? And how can this be done in the context of our contemporary understanding of Christianity? The origins of Christian socialism are not only in

now-dated nineteenth-century social revolt and industrial labour struggles, but also in now-dated nineteenth-
century theology and liberal "social-gospel" biblical interpretation.

Much Christian thinking about politics has proceeded
on a somewhat simplistic assumption that Jesus taught a
useful social ethic – love of neighbour, Sermon on the
Mount, do as you would be done by, a universal ethic of
love, or a socialist society. Thus, Jesus mirrored the liberal do-gooding conscience of the early twentieth century.
But there are real problems with each. Love of God and
neighbour are the basis of all Judaism, and certainly are
not distinctive to nor especially characteristic of Jesus.
The Sermon on the Mount in Matthew and the Sermon on
the Plain in Luke are both addressed to those who are
disciples of the Kingdom (then and now), rather than to all
people in general. "Do as you would be done by" is a
familiar notion among the Cynic philosophers, in whose
image Jesus might well have appeared in Galilee. The
universal ethic of love, again, is urged by all religious
leaders, but the distinctive thing in Jesus is the radical
implications of this in a divided society. And the so-called
socialist society of Jesus is exclusively expected of his
disciples, who are subjected to economic mutual dependence.

I wish to argue that the model of Jesus suggests alternative political stances which are, in fact, more relevant.
But I do not think they can be built on the foundations of
past understandings and assumptions of the Gospels. So,
let us go back to the beginning and try again.

Establishing the Kingdom of God
First of all, Jesus himself needs to be seen as a politician
in his own right, rather than a teacher about political

matters. By politician, I mean someone who is intimately involved, as a citizen, in the affairs of his own time, and who gears his responses, and plans his campaigns, in relation both to some overarching purpose which is being sought, and also to the practical means whereby opposition is to be dealt with, debate entered into, and a few aims actually achieved. Firstly, the "grand design"; secondly, the immediate issues; thirdly, the practical initiatives.

The three elements relate, in fact, rather well to the dilemmas with which we started. Firstly, there is the grand design, the high ground, the overarching aim of Jesus, what I shall call the *Project* of Jesus. Secondly, there is the way Jesus deals with the vicious and unacceptable realities of his time – what I shall call the *Strategy* of Jesus. Thirdly, there is what Jesus actually gets on with, constructively – what I shall call the *Practice* of Jesus.

The Project of Jesus – the thing he announced himself as doing, and which he commits himself to acting out – is the inauguration and proclamation of the Rule of God, the Kingdom of God.

The Strategy of Jesus is how he sets about this Project of the Kingdom, and how he deals with the realities of the day. The Kingdom has to be affirmed, and the Strategy worked out, in relation to the existing social, political, economic, cultural and religious factors of his time.

The Practice of Jesus is how he gets on with some achievable, practical, flesh-and-blood initiatives and actions, in his own life and in the lives of others who relate to him.

Now, let me set out these three elements in clearer and more controversial terms, so that we can see both their usefulness and their challenge to our own political prospects and policies.

The Project of Jesus

The political work of Jesus in AD 30–33 jostles with the options of the political situation of an occupied Province, vulnerable to victimisation and repression by both political and religious forces.

Jesus himself lived in the middle of the Jews' 300-year War for Freedom, beginning with the Maccabean Rebellion in 168 BC, and ending with the revolt of Bar Kochba in AD 132. The Maccabees fought against Greek overlords. The Romans of the first centuries BC and AD were far more vicious. The Romans built ten cities – the Decapolis, set up as fortress towns to exterminate any opposition. Galilee was an enemy-occupied Province. The Roman army's headquarters at Caesarea was the base for the occupying army. Jewish uprisings were ruthlessly put down – 2,000 rebels were crucified a few years before Jesus' ministry. Thirty years after Jesus' death, the great war of AD 66–70 took place. Resistance finally ended in AD 132, with the Rebellion of Bar Kochba. Josephus was the Jewish general in the war of 66–70, who surrendered to the Romans. The *Jewish War*, Chapters 6 and 7, needs to be read with the picture of our Gospels before us.[2] It is a horrifying, vicious, bloody, and ruthless story.

In this context, Jesus declares: "The Kingdom of God, God's rule, God's blessed state, actually is present, right here and now."

The Project of Jesus is to make visible and present the will of the Father that the earth should be restored to its "Original Blessing", as a place in which all living things, and especially all human beings, might blossom and flourish, come into fulness of life, become part of that rightness which the whole of humanity and creation yearns for. If this Project is given the name "Kingdom of God", it means the situation within which the will of God is done, or within which things happen that God approves.

Within this broad purpose, there are two special aspects. First, those who are most separated from the rightness which God intends become the special recipients of attention. The poor have the good news, the captives are released, the blind see, the lame walk, the lepers are cleansed, the outcasts are brought in. Second, the vision of God's wholeness is conveyed by debating its values with those who represent alternative views. The debates with scribes and Pharisees, with those who hold to law rather than humanity, are the classic forms of this. Similarly, the parables are ways in which the sharp edges of God's priorities are asserted against the assumptions of ordinary, rational, culturally or religiously determined prejudices, assumptions and dogmas.

Where is the Kingdom of God?

The Kingdom of God is never defined by Jesus. It is literally "the situation or place which is God's". The Kingdom of God is never "established" as a set place or condition, but it exists where and when certain things happen.

1. Whatever Jesus does in healing or exorcism is part of the Kingdom of God. "If I by the finger of God cast out demons, then the Kingdom of God is here" (Luke 11:20). The Kingdom is the "bringing in" of the sick and excluded.

2. Where there is the wholesale turn round of individuals in a practical sense, there is the Kingdom. Mark has only one basic message: "The right time has come! The Kingdom of God is here. Change yourselves completely. And trust yourselves to the Good News" (Mark 1:15). And this is immediately followed by people who do just that – they leave all and follow (Mark 1:16–20).

3. Where there are temporary manifestations of what

73

the Kingdom represents, there the Kingdom is present. This is the whole meaning of the parables. The Kingdom is suddenly present in otherwise secular activities.

4. The Kingdom is thus hidden within secular actions, Jesus', or disciples', or anyone's. It manifests itself in actions in relation to specific groups. For details, see "Radical Kingdom" in my *Radical Jesus*.[3]

Thus, you cannot build the Kingdom of God. You can await it, expect it, be caught out by it, prepare others for it, hail it in others.

The Project, then, is to get going a situation upon which God can smile, and in which human beings may blossom. Therefore, the Project is not just the setting out of an ideal – it is action on behalf of the disadvantaged, and a sharp critique and exposé of people and situations where the desired state is most oppressed or vitiated.

These aspects of Jesus' activity seem to me to be extremely relevant in our own time. What are the ways in which contemporary flesh is put on the promise of Jesus? The Project of Jesus, in his own time, delineated and embodied as God's Rule, means specific policies in every specific time. Part of our task is to discern and spell them out in our own situation today.

Four slogans

This was the task I attempted in encounters with politicians, both in the House of Commons and in day meetings up and down the country in 1989–90. In the book I used, *Britain in the 90s*, I stated the aim of Jesus in contemporary terms. I took four slogans of our time – Full Life, Enterprise, Initiative and Celebration – and applied some Gospel questions to them. I asked:

The question for Christians must be: What is there in our tradition and distinctive view of things that can provide ways or perspectives whereby we might

1. take the striving for a rich, full life, and apply it to everybody?
2. take "enterprise culture" and "communalise" it, make enterprise more than a selfish pursuit?
3. take the pride in our own private space and home, and make it into pride in our corporate local space and home?
4. take the individualism of diverse cultures, and make a new rainbow out of it?[4]

As a matter of fact, a number of discerning Conservatives observed that this was to take their own slogans very seriously – but then to ask that they be universalised. There is, however, very little possibility for people within political parties to discuss such things, and a "knee-jerk" reaction of defence greets any attempt to do so, all too often. We probably face this problem today among socialists. I venture to think that Jesus faced a similar problem.

Partly, it is the problem of how to deal with realities as they are, when what you really want to do is to make room for some alternative perspectives. Because of the context in which Jesus worked, his main aim might appear to be exposure of existing State and religion. However, he is only *against* what is in power because it is clearly contrary to what he wishes to set up. He is not really interested in the powers of his time, but has to deal with them because they stand in the way of what he really wants to reveal and set up. Those of us who have for years tried to speak on behalf of the needs of Britain's inner cities face a similar problem. We want to talk about the rich possibility of a full life in the inner cities. But all we ever get out is a long and often fruitless groan at the way every policy and almost every government merely conspires to work against us. The *Cry from the Cities* recently published from the Urban Theology Unit is a case in point.[5] But the point I am making must be clear: Jesus' Project is to inaugurate, enact and facilitate the Kingdom of God in his time. Much of his energy, though, is spent in dealing with the problems already present in his society.

Jesus and socialism

So, we have to ask the question: "How does the Project of Jesus, to state and make present God's Kingdom, relate to the project of socialism?"

Socialism was, and is, a system for regulating the political and economic and to some extent the social behaviour of people within a particular kind of developed industrial society. We have to raise the question: "What does the Project of Jesus in establishing the Kingdom of God actually end up in, in our time?" Is the word socialism still useful to us if we are speaking of the Project of God's Kingdom? Has it become, we might even also say, so much a party slogan that it may even prevent some allies joining it?

I recall the first meeting of Christian Organisations for Social, Political and Economic Change in 1970. We debated for an hour whether the word socialist should go into our title. And at the end of the day, the thirty or so organisations concerned with social, political and economic issues from a Christian standpoint decided that they would talk about "change", without saying what they were changing towards. I don't think that is ideal – I just record it as a piece of history.

Socialism has strong values. It has a strong egalitarian implication, which accords with Jesus. But it has not always been faithful to its great perspectives – liberty, equality and fraternity. Nor does it follow the full "programme" of Jesus – which implies a radical humanisation (removal of hierarchies), radical levelling (removal of servant–lord relationships), radical reversals (elevation of "little ones") and radical community (removal of power groups).[6]

In one sense, the Gospel does not go as far as socialism. It does not set up a model for the whole of society based on a Christian viewpoint, or the Sermon on the Mount, or whatever. In this connection, those who describe socialism as the embodiment of Christianity overstate their case.

Indeed, in several important ways the Gospel goes clean beyond socialism. It seems to me that the proclamation and embodiment of the Kingdom of God as the Project of Jesus requires constantly renewed thought from us in our attempt to delineate what in fact the Gospel is seeking to set up as an earthly reality.

At the present time I am working to develop a British theology of liberation.[7] The main line I shall attempt to establish is that the tradition in the Old Testament known as "Jubilee" (see Lev. 25:8–13), or in the Gospel and in British Christian history known as "levelling", is perhaps the way in which we are to embody the Christian project of the Kingdom in achievable terms. Whether or not we are able to use the word socialism to describe what we discern as the Project of Jesus, the task, it seems to me, needs to be done, and needs to be done all over again, and will need to be done again and again in the future.

The Strategy of Jesus

I turn now to the Strategy of Jesus. The activity of Jesus is also significant in his ways of dealing with the actual political realities of his situation. Jesus instinctively, or by design, develops strategies in relation to opposing realities. He is, we may say, a political strategist.

Jesus a political leader?

Firstly, Jesus' strategy is that he goes to the bottom of society. The bottom is not the place where he starts, but the place he moves to. He starts as an aspiring artisan, training to become a rabbi or teacher. But he goes down to the bottom. Jesus becomes the alienated, and the champion of the alienated. He turns his back upon the middle class from which he comes and becomes a friend of outcasts and sinners.

Secondly, Jesus in some sense bypasses the political movements of his time. He belongs to a suppressed group. He acts and speaks as powerless people usually act and speak – with some caution. Thus, politically, Mark's Jesus is a fence-sitter. Take some scenes from Mark's Gospel. He refuses to be associated with leadership of a Zealot-type rebellion, which the five thousand probably expected of him (6:33–44) and out of which he escapes to pray (6:45–46). The people of the time are "like sheep without a shepherd" (6:34). This image of the shepherd is in the Old Testament an image for a political leader. The people are without a political leader, says Jesus. Indeed, it is possible that the role of popular leader is originally what is meant by "the Anointed One", the Messiah (8:29). But this role is intentionally side-stepped. Rather, Jesus seeks to fulfil that of "the Son of humanity" who is to be rejected by the authorities both religious and political – the elders, chief priests and law-teachers (8:31).

So, presented with the problem facing any people under enemy occupation, Jesus refuses to deny the legitimacy of Roman-originating tax and monetary systems. We may recall the well-known saying which we misquote as "Render to Caesar what is Caesar's, and unto God the things of God". What in fact Jesus appears to be saying is: "If you have a coin in your hand, then use your nous. If it is a Jewish coin, use it in the Temple; if it is a Roman coin, then take it to the tax authorities. If the coin is Caesar's, then give it to Caesar; if it is the Temple's then use it in the Temple." (see Mark 12:8–17)

All of this means very clearly that Jesus sits on the fence with regard to many of the pressing issues facing an enemy-occupied country. You either have to say that he is running away from reality; or you have to say that he is not prepared to back either side of problems that are basically not his, and that the thing that he is seeking to set up is in fact more significant than the particular questions relating to attitudes to political and economic realities of his own time. So he bypasses the political movements of his time.

But at the same time, he inevitably is intricately involved in those movements. He takes his terminology and his challenge from them. When he uses the phrase "Take up the cross and follow" (Mark 8:34), it is inconceivable that his hearers would do other than identify what he was saying with the challenge and invitation of the Jewish rebellion movements. It was the rebels who were crucified – it was the political insurgents who took up the cross in his time.

Jesus is not saying, "I am running a Zealot movement." He is saying, "I need the same kind of demanding commitment for the Kingdom which I am setting up, as people have to take up if they are going to become members of the rebel movement." Jesus is starting an alternative movement, and uses the existing political options as ways of formulating the radicality and the totality of the movement that he is inaugurating.

So, thirdly, Jesus must himself have been seen as a political leader in his own time. The terms used in the Gospel for "Master" or "Lord" are indistinguishable from our use of a term like Leader (Führer is the same word). In an enemy-occupied country, everything you say has political implications, has resonances in the political area. Jesus as a leader stands beside other rival political leaders, because of course political in his time means both in the religious and in the national spheres. And, also, you would then have to say that Jesus is a failed political leader. He in the end has to face crucifixion. Was that part of the strategy? Or was it what happens when the strategy fails?

Assuming we in some sense take on the Project of Jesus today, what would it mean to follow his Strategy?

A Christian sharpshooter

One conclusion must be that on the model of Jesus it is OK to "shoot from the hip" – that is, to be a sharpshooter, to be on the look-out for contemporary issues which reveal the endlessly proliferating selfishness and diversions and self-deceits of entrenched vested interests. Now, this also was something, you recall, with which we started. David Ormrod commented about the R. H. Tawney lecture series that many of the contributors had dealt with specific issues, rather than with the question of a final ideal or socialism; that it was easier for Christian socialists to shoot at unemployment or third world debt or monetarism or racism and so on, than it was to deal with larger questions which were in the origins of socialism and in Christian socialism and Christian political thinking. But now we have to say, "OK, we need the sharpshooting." Jesus was a sharpshooter. So were the prophets before him. And there is a need for anyone committed to a large ideal which is unachievable in their time to be on the look-out for everything that goes against that ideal or that achievement.

There is only one proviso. The Christian sharpshooter only operates on the model of Jesus, when the sharpshooting is done from alongside the poor and disadvantaged. This, if I might say it, is probably the greatest problem with British socialists, be they Christian or near-Christian. Within a lifetime, many have risen from being working-class people in industrial areas to being middle-class people in the suburbs. Many Methodists I discover in the south-east of England, who now have jobs as yuppies, grew up in working-class homes in Heckmondwike or Bradford. Both Methodism and socialism have led to upward mobility. This is manifest in the people whom you meet on continental holidays who say, "We're working-class but we did well out of Thatcher." When such people shoot from the hip, they are defending vested interests indistinguishable from the Tories. So there is an even greater problem for us: can socialism as a creed, Christian socialism as a creed, survive among former working-class people whose real and natural interests lie in the preservation of suburbia? For a while, there were ex-working-class teachers and lecturers and social workers and professionals who retained a gut-based commitment to working-class socialism and the Labour Party. But what of the future? Don't you in the end speak from the base – the economic base – that you have secured for yourself?

To journey downwards

Hence the importance of what the liberation theologians call "the Option for the Poor", and what I have called "the Journey Downwards". We need politicians and Christians in our time who will stand beside the poor. Only so can they be trusted to recognise evil when they see it, and only so will their dreams be radical enough to redress the balances set against the poor. Surely it was for this reason that Jesus made his "option for the poor", and became allied to those who were most deprived: so that he could speak alongside them. My question is: "Is a Project for setting up an ideal society credible except through a strategy that places us intentionally alongside the disadvantaged?"

And my question is not simply a romantic journey backwards socially. It is also related to the kind of global society which in future can be sustained. The journey upwards of exponential growth is simply not sustainable globally, in economic, ecological or social terms. Somewhere, all humanity has to start some alternative journeys.

The Practice of Jesus

So, finally, to the Practice of Jesus. What happens to the Project to proclaim and inaugurate the Kingdom in the context in which the Strategy has to be related to the existing powers of religion and society which reveal their opposition to him and to his Project?

Personal and communal change

Basically, what it seems to me that Jesus did, faced with the rejection of his vision and the opposition of its enemies, was not to spend his time writing books, or organising meetings, but to get on with the setting up of a miniature project in the two areas in which he was able to do something. And that is first and foremost in his own life, by himself becoming one who lived amongst the poor; and then in the lives of those who would ally themselves with him, whom the Gospels describe as his disciples and those with him. Thus, the strategy for the situation of rejection is the practice of Jesus in initiating alternative action responses. Jesus just has to do what he can, wherever he can.

Jesus becomes the instigator of radical personal and communal change. He is a pioneer, the bringer of alternative ways, and others get into it as they can. If you are healed, then you are to that extent brought back into the radically different situation. Beyond that, if you want to join the movement – if you want to be a disciple – then you have to adopt the same life style as the leader of the movement. Thus, the disciple group looks like a radical movement, a political movement, a movement of people around and following a radical leader.

There are rules that have to be obeyed within the movement. There is the common life that is imposed upon the members of the movement – they have all things in common, they have a common faith, a common message. They all have to go out and say the same thing: the Kingdom of God is here. They listen to the master, the leader, responding to criticism. They overhear the debates about the policies that are to be carried out. The disciple group is regarded by the leader as of decisive and significant importance. They are the salt within the whole of society – not that the whole of society has to become salt, but that they are the salt within it. They are the leaven within the society – not that the whole of society has to become leaven, but they are the leaven that leavens the whole of society. They are the light – not that the whole of society has to be light, but that there has to be some who are the light within it.

Throughout history, this model has helped Christian disciples by inspiring a preparedness to get on with creating mini-embodiments of the Kingdom of God in our own time, at the same time as holding out the wider vision, at the same time as sharpshooting strategically on behalf of the poor. So, too, we need, today as in every age, the preparedness to get on in our own contexts with our version of socialism or Christian socialism. The model of radical discipleship is a politically relevant one for our time, I have argued recently, in the essays volume, *Religion in Public Life*.[8]

Faith and action

I would go so far as to say that the credibility of socialism or of Christian socialism has been vitiated in our time, not only by the disappearance of the working-class socialists into the suburbs, but also by the absence of prophetic and parabolic action and practice by so-called socialists and so-called Christians. The typical middle-class socialist has become an armchair critic, an armchair reader of books, and an armchair friend of those amongst whom he or she lives in the suburbs. Unless we are able to embody specific parabolic instances and actual examples – mini-societies – of the kind of ideal that we have before us, I do not think we shall be able to project with any credibility a debate about how the whole of society should be run. As I understand the Christian Church, that is exactly what the Church is supposed to be – a place where radical experiments take place which are for the good of all society, and which it would be good if everybody in society did, but which have to be pursued by a small prophetic minority prior to their being taken up by society as a whole. You might say: "Well, if you look at the Church today, heaven forbid that society as a whole should become like the Church. Most churches are a parabolic example of the way that society should not be run!"

The Practice of Jesus therefore suggests for would-be disciples certain sorts of practice for their own time, in relation to the continuing Project and Strategy of Jesus and his disciples, then and now.

Christians in politics are committed to the way of Jesus. Firstly, they are to carry out the Project, to proclaim at every point in history the permanent mandate and the ultimate possibility of the dream, the Utopia, the possibility represented by God's Kingdom, God's will being done, the state of blessing, occasionally actually existing, and always waiting to break out. Secondly, we have to continue the Strategy: to take on the enemies, to expose them, to show their true colours, but to do this in the radical way of Jesus, by being with those at the bottom, and ultimately, if necessary, to be overcome by the powers. For political disciples today, this means doing the contemporary political thing with even more commitment, setting forth alternative possibilities on the basis of our commitment alongside the poor. And, thirdly, we have to continue the practice of Jesus by becoming ourselves citizens and experimental stations of the new reality, by creating in disciple groups miniature outposts of the new society which will have a sharp cutting edge in the whole of society.

Reclaiming the ideal

Tasks for a renewed Christian political consciousness, or a renewed Christian socialism, become clear for the coming decade.

Firstly, there is the need boldly to draw the outlines of a Christian ideal or a Christian nation in the new situations now confronting us, embodying in contemporary form the hopes and possibilities and new realities opened up in the revelation of the Kingdom of God. Theologically and ideologically we must go back to the drawing-board, utilising the new political, social, economic factors of our time – the new Europe, the disappearance of the old east– west, communist–capitalist divisions, the new division between north and south, the reality of a post-industrial society, the futility of technology to deal with the real human problems of our times, the ecological crises of our centuries, the persistence of ancient victimisations based on race, class and gender. What can a vision of the Kingdom be that speaks with those possibilities? That is our challenge and opportunity and invitation.

Secondly, there is need for us as Christians and socialists radically to hold the poor, and work out strategies from the bottom. We must not assume that you can change society from the top; neither must we assume that changes from the top necessarily ever get to the bottom. That has been a mistake of all political parties. We need to see the journey downwards, the option for the poor, as not only an appropriate personal discipline of personal humility and modesty in the face of exploitation and over-consumption, but also a policy ecologically, socially, and technologically vital for the future. We cannot go on with the rapacious attitude of consuming more and more in terms of ecology, society, technology or in terms of personal income. And the journey downwards becomes a new and politically relevant way in which the genius of Jesus' appeal for self-denial becomes an essential part of surviving humanity on our planet. And we must begin to pioneer it.

Thirdly, there is need for us as Christians and socialists again to be the pioneers, ourselves embodying in specific tangible projects and movements the vision of the Kingdom in our own time. Let us make a start.

Building an Equal Society

Let me try, I hope without impertinence, to move these three perspectives even closer to the situation facing Christian socialists in the closing years of our century – and perhaps beyond.

Firstly, we need to keep reflecting on the actual nature of the Project of socialism or Christian socialism. The enterprise of setting up a socialist State was always understood to be a project which would serve the working class. By working class was invariably meant the large number of waged employees, whose lives depended upon their labour which, alongside money and raw materials, formed the staple ingredients in an industrial society. In this situation, a socialist society of whatever sort would clearly benefit workers, by bringing elements of the supply-side of money and materials under the same aegis as the workers' labour.

A Labour Party made sense as being the party which gave voice and power to the vast numbers of wage-earners dependent on the industrial system, promising to bring the other vital elements in the economic system under their control, or at least, into servicing their interests.

Alongside this, however, another element was always present. It was the moral case for an equal society, the crusade to set up such a society, and the compassion and comradeship that such lifelong commitments generated. The origins of this crusade lay in the long traditions of radical Christianity. The socialism of the Labour Party in our lifetimes has been a mix of these two. The Project for a New Society, or a socialist society, has now to be re-created on two new foundations: it has to be built on post-industrial creative human beings whose agenda is not the same as the old working class. It also has to be built on

RECLAIMING THE GROUND

contemporary Christian theology which proceeds less
from doctrines, teachings and dogmas from the New Testament, and more from the dynamic understanding of
Jesus and his activity, which I have attempted to describe.

Secondly, some questions about strategy, which are
also questions of place. Can the principle and hope of a
socialist, egalitarian society survive without the particip-
ation of oppressed groups who stand most to gain from
them? The new middle class, the technological operators
of the computer world, do not have anything to gain from
an egalitarian society. They have only got where they are
by their own skills and expertise, and are now locked into
a costly life style, by mortgages, job dependence, promo-
tion prospects, education concerns for their children, and
work considerations for their spouses. The products of
their labour are not the common needs of the poor, but the
luxuries or assumed necessities of the rich. The early
Labour movement, like the movement of Jesus, was a
movement of certain elements in the social and economic
situation, designed to overthrow palpable enemies. Can
the contemporary would-be socialists be sufficiently distanced from the influences which in fact service their
interests, to be able or willing to identify and oppose
them? Are we not all now so intricately interwoven with
the very structures of our oppression, that only the most
radical of policies or principles would extricate us?

Thirdly, what practice follows? Do we not need to make
some disciples? If the appeal is not to self-interest, the
example of Jesus and his movement might be of more than
passing interest. So let us start proclaiming some new
visions for the future which will be bold and significant
enough to justify some radical personal change and some
radical personal commitment. And for those already committed, there's more. Can a movement survive unless

there are some visible and dramatic instances of its proposals, visible in the public arena for all to see? A movement needs not only people and a vision. It needs also miniature examples of what it is talking about and fighting for. In a time of no consensus, there is work to be done setting up some twenty-first-century garden villages, Port Sunlights, Moravian settlements and Villages in the City. Radical communities in which Christian commonness and socialism can be demonstrated as practical economic and social realities might have to precede any new agreement that a socialist or communitarian system for the nation can again be worked towards. And the histories of both Christian movements and socialist movements suggest that setting up alternative communities is part of the strategy for getting a lever on the future.

BIBLIOGRAPHICAL NOTES

1. David Ormrod (ed.) *Fellowship, Freedom and Equality: Lectures in Memory of R. H. Tawney*, London, Christian Socialist Movement, 1990.
2. Flavius Josephus, *The Jewish War*, E. M. Smallwood (ed.), London, Penguin, 1981.
3. John J. Vincent, *Radical Jesus: the Way of Jesus Then and Now*, Basingstoke, Marshall Pickering, 1986, pp. 27–57. This book is obtainable from the Urban Theology Unit.
4. John J. Vincent, *Britain in the 90s*, Peterborough, Methodist Publishing House, 1989, pp. 5–6.
5. John J. Vincent (ed.) *A Cry from the Cities*, Sheffield, Urban Theology Unit, 1993, and also see John J. Vincent, *Liberation Theology in the Inner City*, Sheffield, Urban Theology Unit, 1992.

6. John J. Vincent, *Britain in the 90s, op. cit.* p. 20.
7. John J. Vincent, *A British Liberation Theology* (forthcoming).
8. Dan Cohn-Sherbok and David MacLellan (eds.), *Religion in Public Life*, London, Macmillan, 1992.

4

The Logic of Community

*Hilary Armstrong is MP for Durham North West, a seat
she has held since 1987. Educated at West Ham College of
Technology, she is Permanent Private Secretary to John
Smith, and an active member of both the Christian Socialist Movement and the Methodist Church. She is also a
member of the National Executive of the Labour Party.*

Most of us usually start reading or writing articles about
Christian socialism with an assumption that it is obvious
why the two aspects of our belief system fit together. We
can usually demonstrate through quotation and practice
why socialism and Christianity are so *obviously* a part of
the same set of moral values. The morality of community
and equality fits snugly with scripture, the life of Jesus
and belief.

But, in 1993, looking at Britain and the last few years
of the twentieth century, I want to start from an opposite
assumption. I want to reflect on the real situation around
me. I spend a lot of my life with socialists and a lot of my
life with Christians. I think it is obvious to me why the two
different beliefs fit together. But, let's be honest, it isn't

that clear to most people. Most Christians would not call themselves socialists, and in Britain most socialists are not Christians.

Despite the fact that I believe the Labour Party does owe more to Methodism than to Marxism, *Tribune* newspaper, in an editorial in October 1992, can describe religious faith as "nonsense" and those who believe in it as "afflicted".[1] So let us start where we are today and explore why so much ground separates Christianity and socialism. Then I shall go on to explore the political condition of Britain today and suggest how Christianity can assist socialism.

Socialism and Atheism

Socialism in this country, more than in those countries that have a developed Marxism in their socialist parties, has matured with a strong, purely moral base. People have become socialists because they felt certain things were right and wrong, and that those feelings were what brought them into politics and kept them there – through the boring meetings and the wet Wednesday canvassing and the sneer of people who think we are stupid for having such a weird hobby. So morality matters to socialists – equally obviously morality matters to Christians. But there the link between underlying assumptions fades.

For socialism also contains not just a mission for morality but also a mission for modernising society, for bringing a rational order to things. Indeed the word rationality is one of the main themes that runs through the aims of socialism both in the *way* in which socialists think they work and in the *aims* of the society that we would like to create. We believe that rationality is in direct opposition to the insanity of the market, or the irrationality of inequality and greed. (Of course I would also say in passing that many of the internal rows between socialists are characterised by much more heated irrationality than you can find anywhere else.)

Now for most people, common sense places rationality and religion in opposition. The drive for rationality in the eighteenth and nineteenth centuries, from the Enlightenment on, was characterised by an assault upon religion not only as a conservative social force, but also as an intellectual force which encouraged irrational explanations for human behaviour. And by resting on faith in miracles, or faith in God above man, much Christianity seemed to oppose rationality as a modernising intellectual force. Therefore, since many socialists are intellectual rationalists they saw Christianity as an opposition – and in some areas and in some ways intellectually it was. The form of knowledge of the one did seem in opposition to the other, and whilst the German sociologist Max Weber could point out the intellectual congruity of the relationship between Protestantism and the rise of capitalist rationality, what counted as the knowledge of faith and rationality did clash. They clashed in people's homes as the world began to be explicable rather than simply mysterious, and they clashed in great socialist novels such as Tressell's *Ragged Trousered Philanthropists*, where religion is posed as deliberately obscuring harsh social realities.[2]

For those whose socialism was driven by Marxism, this antipathy sometimes, though not always, was greater.

Of course this opposition re-created itself, with many Christians feeling "under attack" by socialists for the very nature of their faith. And therefore a further opposition developed. So the simple expectation that because we believe in them both it's obvious why others should is not historically very useful. Rather it is much more likely that there will be intellectual opposition.

Methodism and the Labour Party

How then, despite that opposition of ideas, did the relationship between Methodism and the Labour Party develop? It did so not through ideas or faith, but through the material experience of the Methodist Church. Because Methodism underlined the importance both of the nature of community on earth and of self-improvement, ordinary men and women were assisted not just by the ideas of faith, but by the real experience of community alongside the real experience of self-improvement. For very many working people the Methodist Church was their moral and practical university where they learnt what would now be termed "life skills" as well as faith. People learnt to speak and work through ideas in public, within the organisation they learnt to represent the views and opinions of others, above all they learnt to have the confidence to run their own organisation and for that organisation to work for the community. The development of the Trade Union movement and of the Labour Party in County Durham was much enhanced by the public-speaking skills, the committee work, the basic literacy, that men and women learnt at chapel. My own grandfather, who left school at a tender age and sought work at coal-mines throughout the region and became lodge secretary and county councillor and a highly respected community leader, is a prime example. So ordinary people learnt skills, and they learnt them in the context of improving themselves whilst helping others and building communities. This was the basis on which the Labour Party could build real skills, and real knowledge of how we all might help each other.

So, when we write about the ideas of socialism and Christianity, there are some important oppositions. When we look at the material experiences of, for my Christianity, the Methodist chapels, then the learning of skills brings the two together. Socialism and Christianity are about practices and not just about ideas.

Socialists at Prayer

In looking at the contemporary problems for socialism and for the Labour Party in particular, I want to share two very different religious gatherings – both on the same Sunday in June 1992. The first was in a Roman Catholic church in North London.

A friend of mine's eldest child was receiving his first communion. The church had about a thousand people in it and the forty young eight-year-old first communicants were supported by very many friends and relatives. It was a great occasion. Amongst the communicants' families there were probably over a dozen different nationalities and I suspect over fifty first languages.

Within the church there wasn't simply representation from every continent, but very distinctly different representation from within each continent. It was a genuinely multi-cultural occasion which celebrated not only the Catholicism of everyone there, but also, their life in North London and their success as migrants, as people who had, through hard struggle and in difficult circumstances, improved their lives.

Most of the young people would be going to the same Catholic school next door. Very many of their parents had struggled to survive the traumas of their old country and their host country. Their success in that struggle was there to be seen both in their Catholic celebration together, and in their specific celebration alongside the tens of other nationalities, and in the fact that they had all made it in their new host country. Their Catholicism wasn't just multi-cultural in its background and organisation, it was multi-cultural in the form of its celebration: an English priest, an Irish nun, two African serving boys and a South-East Asian choir.

We had a party afterwards with about seventy to eighty adults, including the deputy leader of the local Labour Council, myself and other Labour people. I would have been surprised if, amongst that population, more than four or five people had voted Conservative. They were working class, but, in 1992, more non-manual workers than manual – as many home owners as council tenants. Not many people were badly off, but not many were at all well off either. There was anxiety about unemployment and yet more cuts in their services and what would happen to us all with another four years of Toryism. But people were not poor.

There was a lot of political talk. We had lost the election – why, and what could be done about it? Surely, Hilary, we weren't going to "water down" our socialism again – what was left? When we talked about politics no one mentioned God. When we were in church no one mentioned socialism. But within both the church and the celebration no one had to. What brought us together and gave us our common language was the joint belief in community – the community of the Church and the community of our socialism.

Now obviously as I am a Methodist there were differences between my Christianity and theirs – as much as there were differences between my socialism and theirs, but the differences didn't matter much, not in the practical experience of community.

The Voters We Must Win

Later on that day we went to a celebration in the Home Counties. A friend of mine from the North-East, the widow of a miner, was celebrating her birthday and her daughter, who had moved to the Home Counties, was hosting the celebration. They were staunch Methodists and most people who came to the party were from the local Methodist church, which had been deprived of its organist for the occasion.

People were in their forties and a bit older and some of their late teen children were there. Christianity was strong, and ran through the way in which we celebrated my friend's birthday, as well as through much of the discussion.

It was another wonderful celebration. The sense of community was very strong. It was practical, and it was alive in nearly every aspect of the occasion. People lived not just for their own families but for each other and the very many others. Nearly every conversation involved, without meaning to, some aspect of the gift of skill, or of how people had contributed to Africa, South-East Asia or another part of the world.

So whilst, in contrast with the earlier celebration, there was no Party involvement, the discussion was all about the politics of community, and whilst there were no different cultures present, the lives of very many people there had involved real work within different communities.

However, people were better off. The average family income would have dwarfed that in North London and for my constituents would have seemed above a king's ransom. But here it was normal. One of the teenagers had a vacation job which paid an hourly wage which was above the average for the whole of my constituents. So materially people were much better off, and it is more than likely that of the seventy to eighty people there probably no more than ten voted Labour.

But their lives were full of community – as full, indeed if not fuller, than the other celebration. They expressed in real practical terms the relationship between Christianity and what I take for socialism. BUT they felt the Labour Party was not for them. And the distance between these good people's lives and the Labour Party was the distance between winning the election and losing it. Without the support of people as close to us as these, then we cannot win.

So what frightened them – certainly not the loss of money from the tax increases to be spent on retirement pensions: they all probably voluntarily gave more than that to charity. No it wasn't the amount but the form of our politics that set them on edge, not our sense of community but the way in which we carried it out which mattered.

Quite simply the Labour Party and, for that matter, British socialism is rather too involved in telling people what to do and how to do it. We are much too little involved in encouraging people through their own activity to create and recreate community. The very Statism of our politics puts such people off completely. And as research has shown in the south-east, people think that our main task in politics is to tell them how to be, and to strip away not just the material advances that they have made but the struggle for their own responsibility and activity in the world.

Love Your Neighbour and Yourself

So, in some way a split has occurred in the way in which the Labour Party has progressed its politics. Many of those who have "got on" through a great deal of hard work and self responsibility seem to feel that we are against them. And these are no stereotypical Essex man and woman here, but people who whilst they are "doing all right" live very strongly within a community. But they feel that our emphasis upon State services and opportunity puts us against their individual responsibility. I don't believe that this feeling of opposition is simply constructed by the media either – since our politics and policy only rarely underline our belief in self responsibility and improvement.

Earlier in this chapter, looking at the way the Methodist Church meshed in with the growth of the Labour Party, I talked about individuals learning skills and learning community together. For these people there was no opposition at all between the hard work of self-improvement and the gift of skill and self to neighbours and the community. In fact quite the opposite, it was easier to learn and improve yourself because it was done in the context of others and the community. But if, to these people, you had suggested that socialism was NOT about self-improvement, they would have thought you were mad. Surely they would have said, "How can we help anyone else if we have no skills, no capacity for hard work and improving our own lot?"

Indeed I want to push this further. If we look not just at the lives of an earlier Labour Party, but also at ourselves, at our own biographies, all of us developed our skills and our selves as fully as we can in order to provide something real in public service. In short there is no value to be gained in simply wanting to create socialism and strong communities if one does not have the personal skills required to put those desires into practice. You need to be self-developed in order to work for social development.

But this relationship has been absent from our policy and politics for some time. It is as if an antipathy has been built up – not just by the Conservatives but by ourselves too – between working for others and working for ourselves. This is a completely false opposition. After all, Jesus quite explicitly enjoined his disciples to fulfil the law by loving their neighbours as themselves, not instead of themselves. Part of the gospel is definitely the genuine love of oneself, born of one's knowledge of the forgiveness and love of God. As the early Christian teacher Irenaeus said, "the glory of God is a person fully alive". We are called, as the children of God, made in God's image, to be fully alive, fully developed and ready to work with God for God's kingdom.

Furthermore the Bible makes it clear that working for others, contributing to the community and sharing the wealth of the earth, all enable individuals to live stronger, healthier, happier lives. The early Church, living at first in fear of the authorities and hiding behind closed doors, soon found a new courage through celebrating their shared communal life in the breaking of bread and drinking of wine. Indeed they found such courage that they could even face martyrdom for their new faith.

So we as individual Christian socialists need constantly to prepare ourselves, develop our skills and ideas. We need to work hard for ourselves and for others. And as a Party we need to fight against the false idea that building a community means denying people the right to do well for themselves. Such an idea is one that cannot be found in Christianity and it is one that should not be found in socialism. If we enter the next election with even a whiff of that antipathy in our policies many people who would really rather like to vote for us will find that they cannot.

So we must always show how both Christianity and socialism bring together self and community development rather than set them against each other, and we must find practical ways of creating a society where individuals build up communities and their community builds up individuals.

BIBLIOGRAPHICAL NOTES

1. *Tribune*, 9 October 1992.
2. Robert Tressell, *Ragged Trousered Philanthropists*, London, Lawrence & Wishart, 1955; n.e. Paladin, 1991.

5

God's Earth

Chris Smith was elected Member of Parliament for Islington South and Finsbury in 1983, and was elected to Labour's Shadow Cabinet in July 1992. He is now Shadow Spokesman on Environmental Protection, and is Chair of the Socialist Environment and Resources Association. Brought up in Scotland, he is a Presbyterian and a Vice-President of the Christian Socialist Movement.

J. H. Muirhead, commenting on Coleridge in 1930, wrote: "'If the bend of a sunlit road, a bar of music, or the glimpse of a face suddenly thrills with romance, it is because these things have brought some unexpected revelation of the value of human life . . . ' I think that this is profoundly true, but it requires to be added that what to the romantic spirit is of chief value in human life is the sense of the infinite which is implicit in it, and is the source of all man's deepest experiences."[1]

The Romantic poets and composers well understood one of the shaping truths of these last two centuries: that the relationship between humankind and the natural world we inhabit matters crucially to our physical well-being, but matters also to the content of our spirituality and to our perception of the divine. Catching glimpses of eternity in the here-and-now is one of the great gifts brought to us by the natural world around us; and in the materialistic flux of modern times it is surely all the more important to hold fast to this realisation.

This is why environmentalism is so important to our modern politics. It is based on a fundamental understanding of the interaction between the human and the natural. As such it is intensely hard-headed, looking at the structure of the natural world and recognising in it the resources and materials we need in order to exist and thrive, and realising moreover the need to use and husband these resources wisely. As well as being hard-headed, however, it helps to enrich our larger vision. It speaks to the soul as well as to the intelligence. Standing in astonishment at the flight of a heron, or a shaft of sunlight thrown across a hillside, tells us something about habitat preservation and land use planning, yes; but for a moment it also enables us – as Wordsworth put it – to "see into the life of things".

A Sense of the Spiritual

For many Christians, this appreciation of the natural world as both material resource and spiritual inspiration forms a core part of their faith. This is not a pantheistic substitution of the natural for the divine; nor is it even a simple adumbration of the cosmological argument for the existence of God; it represents a deeper understanding altogether: the emergence of the infinite in the finite, imperfect but none the less real.

This was for me one of the motivations towards belief. I grew up in Scotland, and spent much of my time – and still do – roaming the hills and mountains of the Highlands. I have struggled through blizzards and peat bogs, staggered along dark stony paths, been cold and wet and drenched and unhappy, but have also lain down in the warm heather in the sun, have stridden across the snow-capped peaks, have looked out over half of Scotland bathed in glorious light.

If I had to identify what it was that beckoned me towards faith, then these experiences in the mountains would most certainly count as a key element. Strangely, they have also intensified my political understanding. There is nothing better than being summarily turned off a piece of mountain land by a landowner complete with gun, ghillies and Range Rover, to stir the rebel blood in me. A lifetime of wandering on mountain and moorland has made me feel passionately about the rights of public access to open country, and how ridiculous it is that private individuals should buy and sell great tracts of God's earth as if they were household chattels. There is a wonderful verse in Woody Guthrie's old song "This Land is Your Land" which tells of how he is walking along a highway and sees a sign saying "Private Land". He looks at the other side of the sign, which says nothing at all, and *that* side, he tells us, is made for you and me.

The Environment Agenda

From the time of the Kinder Trespass, the Independent Labour Party Ramblers and the movement for national parks in the 1940s, there has been a strong thread of enthusiasm for the open air and open access running through the Labour movement's thinking. But the development of environmental politics in recent years has of course gone much further. Environmentalism as we move towards the new century takes a more holistic approach, rightly seeing the environment as a key common component to the whole range of human activity. What we are now beginning to understand – albeit seeing through a glass darkly – is the interconnected way in which the world works, and the very real possibility that humankind could be in the process of destroying those interconnections. God's earth depends for its survival on an intricate pattern of different activities and existences. Are we by our actions threatening to damage – perhaps irreversibly – some of that intricate pattern? This, surely, is becoming one of the defining questions of our modern world. It is up to us to make it one of the defining questions of our politics.

Twenty years ago it would have been impossible even to raise such a question, let alone insist that it should start to shape our public policy. Even in Germany, where environmental politics has advanced far further than it has anywhere else in Europe, such concern has only been a relatively recent phenomenon. Here in Britain, Labour has a reputable record of creating national parks, of promoting clean air legislation, and of insisting on health and safety criteria for the workplace. But the real appreciation of environmental needs as an overarching theme to political life has come only recently and fitfully.

At the time of the European Parliament elections of 1989, the environment was high on the political agenda, rating as a top priority in all the issue polling that was carried out. The Green Party achieved 15 per cent of the vote overall, and in many places did far better than that. Even Mrs Thatcher, who years before had been decrying the environment as humdrum and unexciting, suddenly discovered that at least in her rhetoric she had to start looking and sounding green.

Yet as quickly as the green mood had come, it slipped away again. By the time we reached the general election of 1992 the environment had fallen off the agenda altogether. As Sir Arthur Conan Doyle would have put it, we were faced with the strange case of the disappearing issue. Partly, of course, this was inevitable at a time of severe recession: the concentration was primarily on immediate personal economic prospects, and these dominated political discourse. But we politicians bear a responsibility too: we simply did not raise the environment to the prominence it should have had, both before and during the election. It would be folly for us to assume that it will always be the same. The environment will return to the top of the agenda, where it belongs.

Making the Link

Whilst environmental concern has not surfaced in the electoral politics of the immediate past, it has undoubtedly taken strong root amongst ordinary people. The people are far ahead of their politicians in this respect. They are joining environmental organisations in droves. When it comes to buying products in the supermarket or cosmetics in the High Street or petrol at the filling station, they are making green choices about what they purchase. Sometimes the claims made by manufacturers are entirely bogus, but green consumerism is forcing company after company to change the way they produce, market and dispose of their products. What people do not yet do, however, is to make any close link between that environmental concern and their mainstream politics. We as Christian socialists have to help in the making of that link.

Many Christians through the ages have made precisely that link between their faith and their perception of

107

the natural world. The creation narratives in Genesis, the Wisdom tradition of the Song of Songs and the books of Ruth and Job, Jesus' nature parables and the prologue to the gospel of John, all point to the crucial importance of an environmentally aware spirituality in any response to the God of the Bible, the word made flesh. After all "he was in the beginning with God; all things were made through him, and without him was not anything made that was made" (John 1:2–3 RSV). There is a strong and enduring Christian tradition of consequent thought: the thirteenth-century German Dominican Friar Meister Eckhart, St Francis of Assisi, St Teresa of Avila, Julian of Norwich, and a long history of Celtic spirituality. For all of these what is most significant is a theology far more deeply intertwined with the reality of living in the world; a concern for the environment as a created whole pregnant with the Spirit of God; and a passionate linking of environmental awareness with action for social justice. As Christian socialists these are the themes that should inform our own concern so that we can inform both the Churches in their prophetic role and Government in its political role.

Environmental concern does of course speak directly to our political philosophy as democratic socialists. We believe fundamentally that the dignity of the individual and the well-being of the community are utterly interdependent: that individuals can only become wholly fulfilled when assisted and enfolded by the community of which they are a part; and that the community, the group, or the neighbourhood can only truly succeed if it recognises the unique importance of every individual citizen within it. This interdependence of part and whole is something that only we in the Labour Party understand. And nowhere is it truer or more relevant than in relation to the environment.

The untrammelled operation of the free market – every individual acting alone, for their own interests – never brought environmental protection to anyone. The environment is a common good, to be protected and enhanced by all of us acting together, sometimes potentially diminishing the short-term interests of a particular individual or group so that everyone can benefit. It has of course to be observed that bureaucratic State centralism never achieved environmental advance either – as is painfully obvious from the post-Communist legacy of degradation across the whole of Eastern Europe. To protect the environment in the interests of all you require common decisions, taken and implemented democratically. Leaving everything to its own devices will not work; nor will the imposition of arbitrary decisions. Community and democracy are the key themes – and they are of course the key components of our own political philosophy.

It is too often assumed that environmentalism is about a series of clearly defined, easily identified, discrete "green" issues, somehow set apart from the main core of political thought. Some people think that the environment is about a limited number of issues such as the future of the world's forests, or the state of the ozone layer, or the fate of whales and dolphins, and that these can safely be labelled as "green", wrapped up in recycled paper, and left on one side to be largely forgotten. Nothing could be further from the truth. All of these readily identifiable issues are important, of course; but environmental politics is about so much more as well. It is about the balance of economic activities within the world, about the use of resources and the creation of waste, about the impact of work and production, and about the fundamental welfare of people and the communities in which they live. It runs through every single aspect of our political life.

That is why an environmental approach brings with it a set of attitudes which are every bit as important as the basic issues to which they are applied. These environmental values have to become an integral part of our modern political thinking – indeed in some respects they already are – and they are worth outlining as touchstones for the development of our ideas.

Six Christian Principles

Firstly, environmental concern will always look to the long term. Jesus himself, after all, always admonished his disciples to look to the intimate details of the everyday as a fundamental part of a wider vision. Too often we ourselves tend to ignore this lesson. The speculator on the floor of the foreign currency exchange will think simply of what is likely to happen in the next twenty minutes. Most Western companies look ahead by two or three years at best. Politicians think of the next election in four years' time. Even the most successful Japanese companies – models in their own way of forward thinking – will plan for twenty years ahead. Environmentalism demands that we think not just in decades but in generations. Over the past thirty years we have generated substantial quantities of our electricity from nuclear power, yet the nuclear waste we have thus created will last for centuries, and even now we have no real idea of what to do with it in the meantime. The build-up of sulphur dioxide and nitrogen oxide and hydrocarbons that combine to cause acid rain damage has been accumulating for many years, yet it is only relatively recently that the effect has crossed a threshold of perceptible deterioration. It will take a long time to turn round an impact that has been so long in the making. The environmentalist, therefore, will think far ahead and will weigh carefully the long-term costs against the short-term benefits of any policy option.

Secondly, environmentalism is about the wise use of resources. Jesus tells us the parable of the talents, where the foolish servant wastes the potential of his inheritance by hiding it in the ground, to argue that we are stewards and we shall be held to account for our use of the resources provided to us. So too, St Paul saw us as stewards of the mysteries of God, and "it is required of stewards that they be found trustworthy" (1 Cor. 4:2 RSV). In the earlier stages of industrialisation, no one really questioned whether there might be finite limits to the supply of raw materials or energy. Now, however, we are beginning to understand that we cannot continue blithely to assume that someone somewhere will always provide – especially as the developing world rightly strives to catch up with what we have deemed to call progress in the developed world. We have to husband the resources we know about carefully – and at the same time step up our search for alternative ways of securing the same ends. That is why, for example, the most important task by far in our energy policy is to improve energy efficiency, to invest in programmes of energy conservation, and to reduce our overall consumption. At the same time, we should be researching far more actively into all the potential renewable sources of energy such as wind, wave, and solar power.

Thirdly, an environmental approach will look at the entire life-cycle of a product in assessing its costs, benefits and worth. The opening verses of Ecclesiastes remind us that the world is in a condition of constant and recurring flux, and this recognition should inform the way in which we handle the products of the earth. The raw materials and energy consumed in manufacture, the ease of transport, the waste stream generated, the recycling potential, and so forth: all are important factors and ought to be taken into account. Such a cradle-to-grave assessment is now carried out by many manufacturers, but by no means all. Some for instance still swathe their products in layers of unnecessary packaging in search of presentability and convenience. In Germany the new secondary packaging laws are making supermarkets have large packaging receptacles in the foyer of the store for their customers to strip off the packages and cartons before they leave. The scheme has apparently proved a surprising success.

Fourthly, environmentalism is about taking sensible precautions even when you are not wholly certain of a particular cause and effect: what is known among the *cognoscenti* as the "precautionary principle". As it says in the Proverbs, "The simple believes everything, but the prudent looks where he is going. A wise man is cautious and turns away from evil, but a fool throws off restraint and is careless" (Prov. 14:15–16 RSV). In practical terms, for example, the precise scientific mechanism for the phenomenon of acid rain remains unproved, but most reasonable scientists would agree that sulphur dioxide and nitrogen oxide are undoubted contributors to the problem. Some have argued in the past that the science must be demonstrated beyond peradventure before costly and substantive steps are taken to reduce emissions. Few would argue such a case now. The imperative of reducing emissions has been recognised. The same process of understanding is beginning to take hold with the debate over global warming and climate change. If we wait to prove the links it will be too late. Better to act now to reduce our carbon dioxide emissions, accepting that we do so on the basis of probability rather than proof.

Fifthly, an environmentalist will always consider the

impact, possibly long term, of a particular course of action on others who may be affected by it. Jesus powerfully told us that our own life is intimately involved with that of others around us: "Truly, I say to you, as you did it to one of the least of these my brethren, you did it to me" (Matt. 25:40 RSV). We are called to love our neighbour not just theoretically, but in the hard practical reality of the world as well. So starting up a factory may be a profitable exercise but may in the process create pollution or noise that becomes intolerable for those near by. The balance between profit (and viability) and external impact has to be properly struck. Sometimes, carrying out an industrial process in a quieter or cleaner way may actually turn out to be more profitable. Environmental health officers in Oxford some years ago demanded that a particular paint-spraying operation should cease because of the health impact it was having on those living in the surrounding houses. The company concerned raged at the restriction, saying the entire plant would have to shut down in consequence. In the end, however, a different process was developed which removed all the previously adverse environmental consequences and even worked out as better value for money for the company. The famous BATNEEC principle (best available technology not entailing excessive cost) can work to a firm's advantage, if only it has the courage to try – and to do so because it considers the needs of others as well as of itself.

And sixthly, environmentalism is international in character – because it has to be. The apostles' sudden ability, on the day of Pentecost, to communicate with all the peoples of the then known world reminds us that we do all live on one earth. The environment itself knows no national boundaries: the sea that washes the shores of East Anglia is the same as that which touches the coast of Holland; the air that sits over Chernobyl will at some stage have an impact on Wales. Environmental damage crosses boundaries and affects everyone. It is therefore pre-eminently true that tackling the environmental issues that face us can and must be done on an inter-national basis. Understanding the causes that lead to the destruction of the rain forests in Brazil or the Philippines requires not only a perception of how essential to us all is the "breathing" of the forests and their absorption of carbon dioxide from the atmosphere. It requires also a realisation that the debt crisis created by western loans, and trade difficulties in some cases engineered by Western governments, have helped to force developing countries to turn to the despoliation of their forests as the only hope for immediate survival. Unless and until we tackle properly the issues of trade, development, and debt, we will be nowhere near to solving some of our global environmental crisis – something that affects all of us in the developed West as well.

These six fundamental principles – looking to the long term; using resources wisely; looking at the whole life-cycle; taking precautions; considering always the impact on others; and grasping the need for internationalism – are not simply environmental values, although the rise of environmental politics has thrown them into sharper relief. They are at heart Christian principles and socialist principles too. They would stand as a good *credo* for facing the challenges of a new century.

Turning Theory into Practice

In emphasising a set of values, however, we should not be tempted to decry the importance of specific environmental issues. These are crucial, and will come to dominate political debate in the coming years, whether or not we recognise the need for an environmental approach at a sufficiently early stage. The hole in the ozone layer over Antarctica, for example, is still growing – despite a flurry of international conferences and protocols. Principal among the ozone destroyers are chlorofluorocarbons (CFCs), and Britain has indicated that it will phase these out completely by the end of the decade. So far, so good. But at the same time we are forging ahead with the use of hydrochlorofluorocarbons (HCFCs), which whilst better are none the less damaging. Surely we should be tackling both and not simply replacing the use of one with the other?

A similar case arises in relation to energy policy and the generation of carbon dioxide. Instead of carrying out the intensive work that is needed on energy conservation, with millions of homes crying out for improved insulation and energy efficiency, we are "dashing for gas" and thereby using the precious finite resource of gas in the least environmentally sensible way, to generate power in large plants. It would be far better to use gas on a smaller scale with combined heat and power technology than to use it simply for the generation of large quantities of electricity.

Acid rain damage remains a serious problem, and recent reports have indicated that up to half of Britain's trees may be dying as a result. With the overwhelming consensus now established that sulphur dioxide and nitrogen oxide are the two main culprits, Germany has forged ahead with the "retrofitting" of virtually all of its power stations to remove harmful emissions. It is possible now to remove 90 per cent of the sulphur dioxide by flue-gas desulphurisation, and 80 per cent of the nitrogen oxide by selective catalytic reduction, yet Britain is only retrofitting three power stations, and even that decision had to be wrung out of a reluctant Government after years of trying. New burning techniques such as pressurised fluidised bed combustion could achieve even better reductions, and Britain once led the world in developing the technology at Grimethorpe. The Government closed it down.

A Green Manifesto

Whilst damage to the ozone layer, the prospect of climate change from global warming, and the problems of acid rain may be the largest environmental issues in their global scope, there are many others that are equally important. The trade in toxic waste is of special relevance to those who end up being burdened with its consequences, living next to an incinerator without proper pollution controls or a dump where chemicals leak out over time into the ground and the water-table. The need to treat toxic waste properly, and as near to the point of creation as possible, is important for us all, however. European Community agreements now enable member states to ban the import of toxic waste, and we should do so, except in rare cases of genuine international emergency. We ought also of course to end the export of toxic waste to the developing world: too many loopholes to permit "dumping" still exist. And perhaps most important of all, we should be striving continuously to find ways of minimising the waste stream in the first place.

Meanwhile we should also be changing our patterns of timber use, to ensure that what we use and consume comes from sustainable sources. Some countries such as Holland have already decided that no timber culled from unsustainable sources shall be brought in to the country after 1995. Some British companies – perhaps most notably B & Q – have committed themselves to the same goal, all in aid of protecting the hardwood forests of the world from irreplaceable destruction. Yet the British Government still blandly tells us that it is impossible to identify precisely what the source of a particular piece of timber is, and whether it might be sustainable or not. This is a typical piece of nonsense: if B & Q can trace a timber source, surely the British Government can. It simply requires the political decision and determination to do so.

This Green and Pleasant Land

The principle of sustainability ought not simply to apply to tropical forests. The same safeguards ought quite obviously to exist for temperate regions too. And we should insist that the same approach is taken to our agriculture. For far too long the driving force in European agriculture has been the motivation to overproduce. The Common Agriculture Policy works in precisely this way, and even the recent revisions have not brought with them very much of a change. In the headlong rush for increased production, the values of conservation and the needs of the environment are left behind.

The results are heartbreaking. In the past six years we have lost one fifth of all our hedgerows in England and Wales, precious vital habitats for many of our birds and animals; 95 per cent of the meadows in Northamptonshire have disappeared in fifty years. The number of lapwings in Britain has halved in three decades. The cornflower is almost extinct. Over two hundred sites of special scientific interest are damaged every year. We should not simply continue to plough up more and more land in order to produce food that no one will eat just because the subsidies are there to be claimed. We must begin to do much more to subsidise conservation approaches rather than production approaches to the use of the land.

We should be aware, also, of the close relationship between environmental impact and human health. The air we breathe and the water we drink are vital to our physical health. One of the most worrying aspects of our modern urban life is that the number of children suffering from asthma has doubled in the last ten years. Bronchitis is also sharply on the increase. And these deeply disturbing trends are surely not unconnected with the extent of urban air pollution and the accompanying levels of nitrogen dioxide. Sea water at our bathing beaches can be just as potentially harmful. A recent study by Lancaster University showed that children bathing in the sea at Blackpool had a far higher propensity to subsequent bouts of illness and vomiting than those who didn't go into the water. As we begin – rightly – to see health policy as being every bit as much about illness prevention as about illness treatment, the role the quality of our environment plays in sustaining or undermining good health is a factor that will come increasingly into focus. This will not be before time.

Amongst the list of specific environmental issues, too, must surely be the question of access to the countryside: the issue that first drew me into environmental politics many years ago. Representing as I do the constituency with the least amount of green space of any in the country, I know deep down the sheer importance of access to green space and fresh air for all those who live their everyday lives in densely compacted urban settings. The fact that sometimes such access can be denied by private landowners arouses my wrath in a way that I fervently hope is not unChristian. I find it intolerable, for instance, that large tracts of the Forest of Bowland – fine sweeping

Lancashire moorland in a landscape of wide vistas — should be out of bounds to walkers for the entire year. It is over a hundred years now since James Bryce introduced into Parliament a Bill to give a right of access for the ordinary people of Britain to open mountain and moorland. Sadly, he failed; and there have been a number of unsuccessful subsequent attempts. I long for the day when we can make such legislation a reality, so that the citizens of this country can enjoy our own land to the full.

All of these issues can readily be identified as having environmental relevance; they are self-evidently part of a "green" political agenda. Our environmental approach must however include more, and must underpin the whole range of policy and of government activity, whether automatically seen as falling into a green category or not. Nowhere is this truer than in relation to economic and industrial policy. An understanding of resource use and waste creation ought to be part and parcel of our approach to economic activity. The search must be for a growth that is genuinely sustainable, not secured at the expense of future generations.

Environment and Economics

In earlier times in the Labour movement we tended to see the process of production as being based on a dialectic of opposing forces, the interests of capital outfacing the interests of labour. Such an analysis had substantial merit, and still does. But I believe that we now have to see the production process as a more complex exercise, based on four pillars rather than two: capital and labour, yes, but in addition the interests of the consumer and the needs of the environment. That new understanding brings a profound change to our politics. It makes for less simplistic political appeal, but ultimately for better government.

In recognising the important role of environmental understanding in economic policy-making, we should perhaps begin by appreciating the flaws in our existing measurements of economic performance. The calculation of gross domestic product, for example, takes no account of resource depletion or pollution impact or human cost: it measures productive activity alone. As a secure guide to real long-term economic performance it is therefore inevitably inadequate. At times it can throw up perverse results. When the *Exxon Valdez* went aground off the coast of Alaska, for example, spilling vast quantities of oil over the sea and coastline and causing environmental damage that will last for decades, the costs of cleaning up the mess counted as a plus factor in America's GDP. That cannot be a sensible calculation to make. In order to assess how well or poorly we are performing in real terms – and therefore in order to have the right targets for economic policy to aim at – we must change some of the measurements we make, setting alongside our traditional calculations new indices that do take account of what is happening to resources, energy input, waste and pollution consequences, and environmental impact.

An interesting proposal emerged some time ago from the European Commission which might have begun this process of re-examination and redefinition. Along with the demand that full environmental impact assessments should be made for any substantial planning proposal for the built environment – now accepted, though at times railed against by the British Government – they suggested that the same principle might be applied to governmental policy-making. Environmental impact assessments of all items of Government decision: an idea that might have transformed our political thinking, but sadly not pursued any further. On a smaller scale, we on the Labour benches have consistently argued that the Chancellor of the Exchequer should produce, at the time he announces his Budget decisions each year, a "green book" setting out the environmental consequences of the proposals he is making as well as the "red book" which lists all the financial consequences. The same should of course apply to public expenditure announcements as well as to the Budget, especially when the two become rightly elided into one. The "green book" proposal would have represented a small step in the right direction. It was rejected by the Government.

The same process of environmental impact assessment should, however, be developed not just for government but also for industry and commerce. A system of green auditing to assess the environmental performance of companies, to set alongside more traditional financial accounting exercises, would help to ensure the best possible practices – especially if in due course such a mechanism could be linked to the corporate tax system, to provide a financial inducement for good environmental behaviour. The question should constantly be being posed: can any of these company processes and activities be carried out with better environmental impact, and at acceptable cost? Too often at present the question is not even asked, let alone answered. A system of auditing could ensure that pressure is maintained so that the issue of best practice is always addressed.

Regulation, Incentives and Rights

It is too frequently assumed that improved environmental behaviour automatically costs money and destroys jobs. As in the Oxford environmental health case, companies often find that – having started out being heavily sceptical of changed procedures or the use of different materials – when the new ways of working are actually in place, the change has benefited the company in traditional financial terms as well as in environmental terms. This is not always the case, however, and there may indeed be occasions on which the option of better practice does entail greater cost. It was ever thus. The fight for better standards of employment, shorter working hours, an end to child labour, equal pay for equal work, or proper standards of safety in the workplace, has always involved the prospect of greater expense for the employer. Improved behaviour, however, pays for itself over time in improved performance, wider public acceptance, and ultimately better market share. It is often quality of production rather than simple cheapness of operation that matters in the end; undercutting everyone else's standards does not ultimately lead to the absorption of their markets. The industrial performance of Germany during the 1980s is a classic case in point: relatively high wages, strong worker involvement in decision-making, and high standards of environmental protection, led not to diminished but to enhanced economic performance.

Nor should it be forgotten that action for environmental improvement has the capacity to generate employment in its own right. If we had had a coherent programme in Britain to retrofit our power stations to remove sulphur dioxide – much of the technology for which originated here – there would have been not simply national opportunities for desulphurisation work, but international possibilities too. The catalytic converter was a British invention, but we have almost wholly failed to exploit the market it has opened up. There is a crying need for a national programme of energy efficiency work to insulate homes up and down the country, which could create employment, reduce household bills, and reduce our carbon dioxide emissions all at the same time, yet there has been no real sign of Government interest or activity of this kind. Meanwhile our public transport infrastructure crumbles to pieces, and we invest far too little in its maintenance or development. Environmental work is there to be done, improving our quality of life, generating jobs, and providing the catalyst for further economic activity. We should not regard the imperatives of environmental improvement as simple negatives seeking always to restrict the actions of companies or individuals, but as positive opportunities for development in different ways and new directions.

Whilst the process of proper regulation to ensure environmental protection must always remain the linchpin of policy, there is of course much scope for the use of economic incentives too. When the Conservatives talk of using economic instruments to change environmental behaviour, they invariably mean placing almost total reliance on the operation of market forces to do the trick. Market forces will most certainly not achieve success if left to themselves; but we can surely explore ways in which financial or fiscal incentives and discouragements can be used to complement the framework of regulatory control. When a differential was introduced in the level of duty imposed on unleaded petrol, usage shot from 2 per cent to 30 per cent within months. The same principle can be applied across much of our taxation system, helping to bring about changes in behaviour by means of VAT inducements, or vehicle excise duty changes, or amendments to company car taxation, or the introduction of levies on landfill. And surely we should also explore some wider issues, considering the possibilities opened up by the taxation of non-renewable resource use, or waste or pollution creation, rather than maintaining the focus of taxation on income and work? There are new ideas here which deserve clear-eyed consideration, weighing up all the social and fiscal consequences, but which might well serve to make a valuable contribution to the democratic socialist project.

Alongside the system of national or local regulation and of fiscal incentives, however, should be established a third arm of policy to achieve environmental objectives. We should institute a network of individual environmental rights for citizens, who can then themselves exercise their own rights to secure environmental improvement. A right to air of a particular quality, water that is safe, or a workplace that is healthy, set in the context of a basic right to information about what is happening to our own environment, could for the first time place substantial power in the hands of ordinary people to seek redress or insist on better performance. An essential part of any such framework of rights – which should ideally be instituted on a European rather than simply a British scale – would of course have to be accessible means to exercise the rights in practice. Relying simply on court procedures would be inadequate, given the difficulty, cost and daunting nature of legal action. A number of ideas could be explored: a special environmental court adapted to the needs of the litigant; or an environmental ombudsman; or perhaps a "green Commissioner" based on the model of the Trades Union Commissioner but here used for virtuous purposes, acting on behalf of the aggrieved citizen to secure environmental action. Rights to a safe and sustaining environment, coupled with the readily available means to secure them, could in truth transform the quality of life for us all.

Lilies of the Field

Environmental politics, after all, is not an optional extra to be bolted on to our mainstream values and ideas in order to court a potential "green" vote. Environmentalism must be an integral part of our vision of a saner, safer, fairer way of organising ourselves as a society. The scale of the environmental crisis cannot be over-stressed. Globally we are losing 3,000 square metres of forest every second. Ten plant and animal species are extinguished every day. Half of our British trees are damaged by acid rain. The air our children breathe is full of pollutants as never before. For centuries our world has been a place where an intricate ecological balance has danced in a beautiful pattern to delight the human senses and enhance our physical and emotional lives. We now have to face up to the very real possibility that our own actions may be destroying precisely that intricate balance that ultimately sustains us. Human mismanagement may well be having an impact on God's creation that we never intended, never dreamed of, and still have difficulty in acknowledging. Yet acknowledge it we must if our politics is to have any real or ethical substance as we approach the twenty-first century. Improving the lives of all cannot conceivably be done without looking to the environmental needs by which we are all surrounded and in which we all share.

William Blake put words into the mouth of Isaiah in *The Marriage of Heaven and Hell*: "I saw no God, nor heard any, in a finite organical perception; but my senses discover'd the infinite in every thing, and as I was then persuaded, & remain confirm'd, that the voice of honest indignation is the voice of God, I cared not for consequences, but wrote." Discovering the infinite in the

125

everyday ecological organisation of our earth, and speaking for its needs with a voice of honest indignation, is surely one of the highest purposes of our politics.

"Consider the lilies of the field, how they grow; they toil not, neither do they spin: And yet I say unto you, That even Solomon in all his glory was not arrayed like one of these" (Matt. 6:28–29 KJV). And let us also ask ourselves this: What will our world be worth if there are no longer any lilies of the field left within it?

BIBLIOGRAPHICAL NOTES

1. J. H. Muirhead, *Coleridge as Philosopher*, London, George Allen & Unwin, 1930, p. 28.

6

Reclaiming the Ground – Freedom and the Value of Society

John Smith has been a Member of Parliament since 1970 (Lanarkshire North 1970–83, Monklands East since 1983). A lawyer by training, he is a Queen's Counsel. Having played a vital role as Shadow Chancellor in the run-up to the 1992 general election, in July he was elected Leader of the Labour Party by an overwhelming majority. He is a member of the Christian Socialist Movement and the Church of Scotland.

R. H. Tawney was throughout the whole of his long and productive life an uncompromising ethical socialist. He founded his political outlook on the moral principles of his Christian commitment. From that strong redoubt he assailed the deficiencies of both communism and capitalism and espoused the cause of a democratic socialism. This sought to enhance individual freedom in a framework of collective common purpose and opportunity, in which fellowship was the bond of a community of equality. He saw British socialism as ethical, individualistic, parliamentary and pragmatic.[1]

127

Were he alive today, I do not think he would have been surprised by the failure of communism, or the disillusionment at the results of unrestrained market forces. Throughout his life he was a vigorous opponent of both ideologies, both of which he saw as antithetic to his vision of a society founded on fraternity and solidarity.

His Christian faith, which I am glad to share, was the foundation of his approach. But he did not claim – nor should any Christian – that only Christianity could provide the moral framework for an ethical approach to politics. Our own experience tells us that an ethical approach to life and politics can be held as firmly by people of other faiths and by those who hold no religious conviction. Nor should Christian socialists ever seek to suggest that Christians must be socialists. Because we, like Tawney, see our Christian faith as leading towards democratic socialist convictions, we must always recognise that fellow Christians might properly arrive at different conclusions from ourselves.

Christian Principles and Public Policy

With these necessary qualifications in place, let me assert my profound conviction that politics ought to be a moral activity and we should never feel inhibited in stressing the moral basis of our approach. Of course, we have to take matters further forward. We have to undertake the intellectual task of applying a moral principle in a way which results in a practical policy of benefit to our fellow citizens. And life is never free of dilemmas. But let us never be fearful of saying that we espouse a policy because it is, quite simply, the right thing to do. And let us not underestimate the desire, which I believe is growing in our society, for a politics based on principle.

What is more, I believe the tide of opinion is beginning to flow towards a recognition of the value of society and away from the nihilistic individualism of so much of modern Conservatism.

Archbishop William Temple

Fifty years ago there was such a recognition as, in the throes of a World War, two major thinkers were reflecting on the needs of a nation. Beveridge, whose seminal report was the basis of the social action programme of the great post-war Labour Government, called for a war against the five giants of want, disease, ignorance, squalor, and idleness. At the same time, William Temple, Archbishop of Canterbury, published *Christianity and the Social Order* which strongly asserted the duty of the Christian churches to concern themselves with the application of Christian principles to the needs and problems of society.

Temple did not advocate a Christian social ideal: indeed he was sceptical about ideal States from Plato onwards. But he believed Christianity could provide something of far more value – namely principles which could guide our action. He identified three guiding social principles – freedom, fellowship and service.

Freedom, for Temple, meant freedom "for" something as well as freedom "from" something, and was the primary object of all political action. But he recognised that human beings are naturally and incurably social, and freedom is best expressed in fellowship. The combination of freedom and fellowship resulted in the obligation of service; service to family, to community and to nation.

Temple drew an important distinction between personality and individuality. "Every person is an individual, but his individuality is what marks him off from others; it is a principle of division; whereas personality is social, and only in his social relationships can a man be a person . . . This point has great political importance: for these relationships exist in the whole network of communities and associations and fellowships. It is in these that the real wealth of human life consists."[2]

The theme that unites the writings of Tawney and Temple and which makes them so appealing to democratic socialists is their insistence on situating the individual in society. Individual freedom for them is only meaningful and achievable within society. This explanation of human experience is, of course, a core belief of democratic socialism. It provides an organising principle around which we believe our social order both political and economic can and should be built. It is the way in which we believe that individual freedom – our ultimate moral goal – can best be secured.

A Post-Thatcherite Agenda

In what follows, I will try to explain why I believe that real freedom depends on the interdependence of the individual and society, and why this idea – which has long remained at the centre of democratic socialist thinking – retains its intellectual force and its capacity for popular appeal.

For despite the considerable electoral disappointments that many parties of the left have experienced in Western democratic societies throughout the 1980s, there remains strong public acceptance for many of the principles and achievements of democratic socialism. I am thinking in particular about the National Health Service in Britain and the framework of social and employment rights that are widely supported in most countries in Western Europe.

Indeed it is surely a paradox that despite their electoral achievements since 1979, the Conservatives have really achieved so little in reshaping public attitudes in their own *laissez-faire* self-image. The Thatcher revolution in this respect is looking far less revolutionary today – particularly as John Major's Conservative Party struggles to find a post-Thatcherite agenda amidst the economic and social ruin that thirteen years of Tory rule have brought.

Our Neo-classical Roots

What I believe to be certain is that the flaws in the free-market doctrines of the radical Right are becoming more widely appreciated and more easily exposed than ever before. Their vision of humanity consists of individuals as decision-making units, concerned exclusively with their own self-interest, making transactions in a marketplace. It is a theory which makes very ambitious moral and economic claims; for example, that it alone preserves freedom and promotes prosperity. I believe, however, that it is a doctrine based on an absurd caricature of human behaviour, which grossly misunderstands the nature of freedom, and seriously ignores the value of society – even to the extent of denying its very existence.

Its roots go back to the neo-classical writers of the eighteenth century – to utilitarians like Jeremy Bentham who argued that human conduct is solely motivated by the pursuit of pleasure and the avoidance of pain, and who believed that "The community is a fictitious body, composed of . . . individual persons."[3] A comment to be compared with Mrs Thatcher's notorious remark that there is "no such thing as society". Here, if proof were needed, is conclusive evidence to support John Maynard Keynes' famous warning about the power of the ideas of economists and political philosophers "both when they are wrong and when they are right" to influence future generations. "Madmen in authority," wrote Keynes, "who hear voices in the air, are distilling their frenzy from some academic scribbler of a few years back."[4] In such a fashion were the extreme anti-government polemics of Friedrich Hayek disinterred from near-oblivion to be put to the service of Mrs Thatcher, Keith Joseph and others.

The fundamental flaw in the individualism of the neo-classical writers and their modern counterparts in today's Conservative Party is, I believe, their assumption that human beings conduct their lives on the basis of self-interested decisions taken in radical isolation from others. This thesis grotesquely ignores the intrinsically social nature of human beings and fails to recognise the capability that all people have to act in response to commitments and beliefs that clearly transcend any narrow calculation of personal advantage.

Of course, people have a natural and powerful regard for their own interests and that of their families. That is certainly a dominant and entirely necessary feature of human experience. As Archbishop Temple warned, "a statesman who supposes that a mass of citizens can be governed without appeal to their self-interest is living in a dreamland and is a public menace" (adding the wise advice that "the art of government in fact is the art of so ordering life that self-interest prompts what justice demands"). But although Temple accepted that "man is self-centred" he also believed that "this is not the real truth of his nature. He has to his credit both capacities and achievements that could never be derived from self-interest."[5]

Re-reading Adam Smith

Providing perhaps unexpected support for this line of argument is none other than Adam Smith who in the *Theory of Moral Sentiments* wrote: "How selfish so ever man may be supposed, there are evidently some principles in his nature, which interest him in the fortune of others, and render their happiness to be necessary to him".[6] The fact that this insight of Smith's is difficult to reconcile with his later and more famous study of economics has caused many of his recent followers to overlook his earlier work. Just as they also tend to ignore his support for public investment in infrastructure, in education and the arts which are hidden gems of intervention that can be found alongside his thesis of the invisible hand in the Wealth of Nations.[7]

Human beings are therefore, I believe, much more than the "*Homo economicus*" of neo-classical theory. They are people living in families, in communities, in regions, and in nations. People sharing languages and cultures which in themselves shape our aspirations and ideals. People living in societies which profoundly affect our individual ability not merely to make commercial transactions, but to co-operate in ways which crucially determine our capacity for personal freedom and spiritual fulfilment. In Temple's words we are not just individuals but also personalities.

Similarly markets do not enjoy the total supremacy that is envisaged for them by neo-classical economics. Market systems, whilst remaining an effective and useful means of enabling choice and distribution of myriad goods and services, exist alongside and are embedded in other social and political institutions which also contribute to human welfare, and which themselves shape and modify the way markets actually work.

Community

Implicit within so much *laissez-faire* theory is the idea that a perfectly functioning unregulated market is the natural state of humankind. And that this system has occurred somehow spontaneously "as if economic man was a biological–psychological miracle, born fully formed, say in his mid-twenties with his preferences 'immaculately conceived'."[8]

The truth, of course, is that markets are social institutions created within communities that have already developed complex structures of co-operation and common identity; structures which have been characteristic features of human existence from the earliest days of civilisation to our own modern-day industrial democracies. And it is within these civil institutions, held together by bonds of mutual trust and consent – absolutely crucial elements of human co-operation – that the business of markets is able to take place at all.

It surely follows that if the neo-classical explanation of both human behaviour and of markets is seriously flawed, then, I believe, so are the political and economic systems that are erected upon it. That is why, in my view, the modern Conservative conception of individual freedom is so incomplete and the role they ascribe to government is so inadequate. For it is upon these same neo-classical assumptions that they adopt a highly restrictive conception of what it is to be free and they base their case for radically limiting the role of government. Hence we arrive at the model of a minimal State – in its most idealised form with the authority only to protect property rights and enforcement of contracts of exchange.

If, as I profoundly believe, the moral goal of our society is to extend and encourage individual freedom, then it is certainly not enough to rely simply on a minimal State charged with defending negative liberty – the freedom from coercion by the State. For as Tawney himself observed, "A society, or a large part of it, may be both politically free and economically the opposite. It may be protected against arbitrary action by the agents of government, and be without the security from economic oppression which corresponds to civil liberty."[9]

Citizenship

What Tawney realised was that meaningful freedom depended on real ability. That for millions of people citizenship was empty and valueless if squalor and deprivation were the reality of a society only theoretically free. What was needed was positive liberty – the freedom to achieve that is gained through education, health care, housing and employment. An infrastructure of freedom that would require collective provision of basic needs through an enabling State. It is this richer conception of freedom for the individual in society that is the moral basis of democratic socialism.

It is also a vital theory of citizenship, just as concerned as any neo-classical writer with protection from coercion by the State and with the values of democracy. And, of course, in this important respect it is sharply distinguishable from the anti-democratic and totalitarian forms of socialism against which Tawney was such a steadfast opponent.

For Tawney Marxism was a "barbarous inhuman sordid doctrine" as amoral and materialistic as *laissez-faire* capitalism. He was scornful of those who believed that the Labour Party had something to learn from Marxist collectivism, accusing its supporters of a "credulity so extreme as to require, not argument, but a doctor."[10] He saw quite clearly that liberty-creating socialism was only possible in a context of political democracy and freedom of speech and thought. After the collapse of the former Soviet Union and its satellites, I think Tawney is shown to have had an insight and a percipience which saw through the deterministic philosophies which took so little account of the moral influences on humanity.

It would also, I am sure, be a considerable source of pleasure to Tawney if he were alive today, to know that his arguments for social justice, freedom and democracy retain all their persuasive power even after a decade dominated by Conservative ideology. For despite the supreme arrogance of their period in government, the so-called triumph of Thatcherism and the radical Right has been remarkably short-lived. Its narrow conception of freedom and its adamant support for unfettered free markets is being challenged not merely by traditional opponents such as the Labour Party but from within its own ranks.

Winning the Argument

A striking example of this trend was the publication last year by the Institute of Economic Affairs of a study by the Oxford philosopher John Gray entitled *The Moral Foundations of Market Institutions*. Gray, previously closely associated with the ideas of the New Right, now argues that freedom requires the creation of an enabling State, meeting the basic needs of its citizens and which is modelled on European (particularly German) ideas of a social-market economy. His IEA pamphlet, deploying arguments not unfamiliar to Tawney, exposes the inadequacy of negative liberty as advocated by supporters of *laissez-faire* capitalism and offers in its place as "the only principled position" an enabling Welfare State "which confers on people a variety of claims to goods, services and resources."[11]

To be fair to Gray's work I should add that he is critical too of the egalitarian arguments of democratic socialists. He is dismissive of concerns about fairness and social justice on the grounds that, in his view, the basic needs that are necessary for individual freedom are readily satiable. This is a critical and controversial point of debate which is disputed in an interesting commentary on Gray's paper written by Raymond Plant and which the IEA have helpfully included in their publication.

I believe it is significant that some honest advocates of the radical Right are having to come to terms with the limitations of their theories and that this is just another sign that the intellectual ground is moving steadily towards the democratic Left.

Moral Foundations for Christian Socialists

The conclusion I reach is that the goal of individual freedom and the value of society, which we advocate as democratic socialists, is a theory of sustained intellectual force. When tested in the experience of humanity it can be found to be a better explanation of the lives and purposes of men and women than its rivals on the *laissez-faire* Right or the Marxist Left. We ought therefore, in the battle of ideas which is at the centre of the political struggle, to be confident in the strength of our intellectual case.

But I believe we must also argue for our cause on the basis of its moral foundation. It is a sense of revulsion at injustice and poverty and denied opportunity, whether at home or abroad, which impels people to work for a better world, to become, as in our case, democratic socialists. The powerful contribution of Christian socialists in all the denominations of the Church has always focused on the moral purpose of political action. How true it is that the Labour Party has owed more to Methodism than to Marx. But it was that great Anglican, William Temple, who identified what he called "the real wealth of human life", who saw that the individual was best fulfilled in the context of a strong community bound together in fellowship. That is a truth I want to re-assert today with confidence and conviction. It is why I believe the Labour Party must be bold in demonstrating our commitment to enhance and extend individual freedom by building a society which is dynamic and responsive to the aspirations of all our people.

Family, Community and Nation

Temple defined the relationships which constituted our real wealth as existing in terms of family, community and nation. We ought to support family life as one of the foundation stones of a good society and in consequence fight determinedly against the unemployment, poverty and lack of opportunity by which it is so often menaced. When Labour founded the National Health Service we lifted a great burden from the shoulders of ordinary families who were set free from the financial perils of ill health.

In 1993 we ought to reflect that in this year a new American President is following in the footsteps of a pioneering Labour government forty-five years ago. Let no one tell me that the principles of democratic socialism – of which the NHS is a fine example – are dated. They are, as in this comparative example, often ahead of their time.

By the same token we must strengthen our communities and our sense of community. The undermining of local government (which is part of the deliberate downgrading of all alternative power systems to the central State) means that communities are being weakened by having no means to advance their own ambitions and to tackle their own problems in their own way. That is why I urge a renaissance of local government in the context of a more pluralistic and diverse society. It is why I believe that devolving power from an overcentralised Westminster and Whitehall to Scotland, Wales, and the regions of England is a necessary part of the refurbishment of our democracy. Democracy has to be a vital and constantly refreshing element in our socialism.

Obligations for Christians and Socialists

We want also to build a society which strives always to unlock the talent and skills of its own people, to harness what Tawney once magnificently described as "the extraordinary potential of ordinary people". More and more we realise, as deskilling and lack of training inhibit our economic capacity, that a policy of social opportunity also makes the most obvious economic sense.

As we near the end of the twentieth century our horizons must extend well beyond our own national frontiers, to our new relationships which are developing fast in the European Community and to our obligations and opportunities in the exciting, but often perilous circumstances of the post Cold War world. Thanks be to God that we now perhaps have the opportunity of diverting our resources from the piling up of armaments which threaten our planet's existence, to tackling the profound injustices and deprivations of the North/South divide. There is no doubt whatever where our obligations lie both as Christians and as socialists. We must never allow the needs of the developing world, where live the majority of our fellow world citizens, to be anything but central to our political purposes. There is no good reason why Britain should not have emulated the achievements of the Scandinavian countries who, profoundly influenced by their social democratic tradition, have set standards which in recent years our country has fallen well below.

In Britain and the world of the new century which approaches we will need to give the enhancement and protection of our environment a prominence which simply did not enter into the consciousness of earlier generations. The earth upon which God has placed us should be for us a special trust from one generation to another. The need to develop effective action to implement that trust is a dramatic illustration of how economic forces need to be contained and controlled for the good of the world community right across both frontiers and generations.

Hope for the Future

We ought to approach our politics with a sense of optimism for the future. There is so much of good that can be done if we seize the opportunities which a modern world makes available. Instead of carrying the miserable burden of mass unemployment, we could be investing in new technology and in new skills, training and retraining our talented people to face a fiercely competitive world: instead of our education system declining and our health service fracturing, we could be building high-quality public services which extend security and opportunity to every family in the land; instead of a society diminished by the violence and dishonesty of crime, we could be building strong communities which provided opportunity as well as protection for every citizen. There is so much we can do; there is so much we need to do.

The second commandment calls upon us to love our neighbours as ourselves. It does not expect a frail humanity to be capable of loving our neighbours more than ourselves: that would be a task of saintly dimension. But I do not believe we can truly follow that great commandment unless we have a concept of care and concern for our fellow citizens which is reflected in the organisation of our society. In this vital way we can ally our Christian faith to our democratic socialist conviction. In the pursuit of both we can aspire to lead our country to find the real wealth which only a good society can provide.

BIBLIOGRAPHICAL NOTES

1. Dennis and Halsey, *English Ethical Socialism*, Oxford, Clarendon Press, 1988, p. 245.
2. William Temple, *Christianity and the Social Order*, London, Penguin Special, 1942.
3. Jeremy Bentham, *An Introduction to the Principles of Morals and Legislation: A Fragment on Government* (ed. W. Harrison), Oxford, Blackwell, 1960.
4. John Maynard Keynes, *General Theory of Employment, Interest and Money*, London, Papermac, 1963.
5. William Temple, *op. cit.* p. 65.
6. Adam Smith, *The Theory of Moral Sentiments* (1759), Oxford, Clarendon Press, 1976.
7. Adam Smith, *The Wealth of Nations* (1776), New York, Modern Library Edition, Random House, 1937.
8. Amitai Etzioni, *The Moral Dimension – Towards a New Economics*, New York, Free Press, 1988, p. 10.

9. R. H. Tawney, *Equality*, London, George Allen & Unwin, 1931, p. 244.
10. R. H. Tawney, *Radical Transition*, p. 158, cited in Dennis and Halsey, *op. cit.*
11. John Gray, *The Moral Foundation of Market Institutions*, London, Institute of Economic Affairs, 1992.